The Book of American Trade Marks, Volume 4

# TradeMarks/4

## The Annual of Trade Mark Design T.M.

# David E. Carter

Century Communications Unlimited, Inc.

Post Office Box 591    Ashland, Kentucky 41101

Century Communications Unlimited, Inc.
1500 Carter Avenue, P.O. Box 591
Ashland, Kentucky 41101

Library of Congress Catalog Card Number: 72-76493
International Standard Book Number: 0-915642-04-2
ISBN for Standing Orders for this series: 0-915642-00-X

# How to submit marks for future volumes.

*The Book of American Trade Marks* is an annual publication, showing good examples of contemporary trade mark design.

Designers are invited to submit marks for possible inclusion in future volumes. Work submitted should adhere to the following guidelines:

(1) if at all possible, send the marks in the *actual size* they are to be reproduced in the book. This will permit your print to be used directly on the paste-up, and will assure that your mark reproduces well in the book.

(2) do *not* mount the work.

(3) include the name of the client, and the way you wish to be identified in the credit line. Include your address for the index.

(4) send a letter giving permission for the marks to be included in the book.

Materials sent will be acknowledged only if a stamped, self-addressed envelope is included.

Designers who have three or more marks included in any one volume will receive a free copy of that volume. Those with one or two marks selected will be given the opportunity to purchase copies at a greatly reduced price.

All material should be sent to: David E. Carter, Century Communications, Inc., P.O. Box 591, Ashland, Kentucky 41101.

This book is dedicated to E. D. Mittendorf, who as Editor of *The Russell Times,* served a small community as a journalist and as a humanitarian.

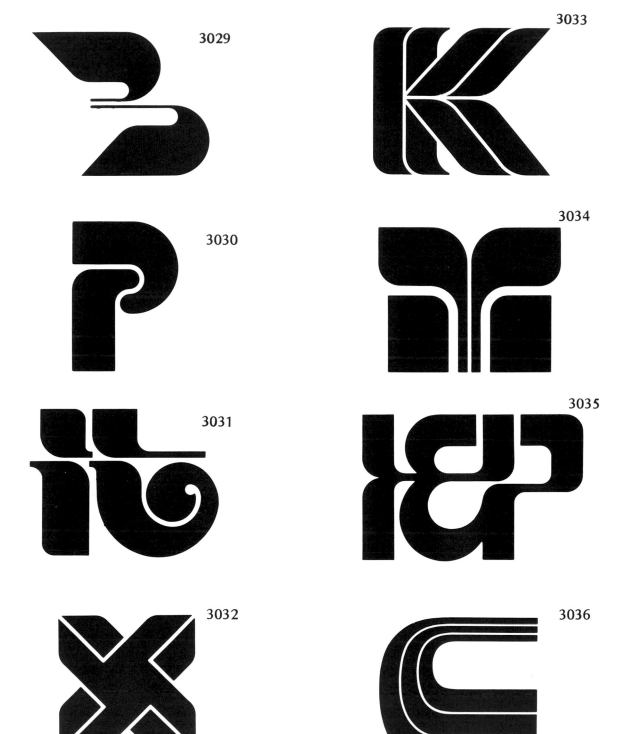

3029

3033

3030

3034

3031

3035

3032

3036

3037

3038

3039

3029  Bradford-Pittman Travel
       Designer: James L. Potocki

3030  Woodland Hills
       Designer: James L. Potocki

3031  IT Cosmetics
       Designer: James L. Potocki

3032  Compass Computer Services
       Designer: Bruce Cockerill;
           James Potocki & Associates

3033  Keystone Mortgage Co.
       Designer: James L. Potocki

3034  The McDonald Company
       Designer: Paul Holmquist,
           James Potocki & Associates

3035  Huttas and Potocki
       Designer: Paul Holmquist;
           James Potocki & Associates

3036  Community Cablevision Company
       Designer: James Potocki/Roy Ritola

3037  Unicorn Systems Company
       Designer: James Potocki

3038  Carlsberg Financial
       Designer: James Potocki

3039  Liquidity Fund Inc.
       Designer: James Potocki;
           Huerta Design Associates

 3040

 3044

# Kangaroo 3041

# CONCEPT 3042

# sDParkERCOMPanY 3043

**NORTHWEST PIPELINE CORPORATION**

3045

3046

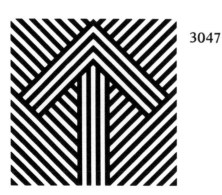

3047

3040 Management Accounting Package/Unicorn
Designer: James Potocki;
James Potocki & Associates

3041 Kangaroo Campers
Designer: James Potocki;
James Potocki & Associates

3042 Concept
Designer: James Potocki;
James Potocki & Associates

3043 S.D. Parker Co.
Designer: James Potocki;
James Potocki & Associates

3044 National Credit Information Service
Designer: James Potocki;
Huerta Design Associates

3045 Northwest Pipeline Corporation
Designer: Reeves, Dyke and Co.

3046 Seaton Industries
Designer: E.W. Baker, Inc.

3047 Houston/Ritz/Cohen/Jagoda
Designer: Wayne Houston

3048 The LTV Corporation
Designer: Walter Landor Associates

THE LTV CORPORATION

3048

 3049

 3053

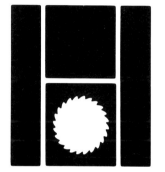 3050

 3054

 3051

 3055

 3052

ALLIS-CHALMERS

3056

 3057

 3058

 3059

 3060

3049  Hill Acme Company
      Designer: Evan Kiousis

3050  Loma Machine & Mfg. Co.
      Designer: Evan Kiousis

3051  Sherwood Selpac Co.
      Designer: Evan Kiousis

3052  Allis-Chalmers
      Designer: Gerald Stahl

3053  Harris Trust and Savings Bank
      Designer: Schecter and Luth

3054  Terrace View Apartments
      Designer: Harvey C. Dellinger

3055  Mission Hill
      Designer: Harvey C. Dellinger

3056  Haymarket Square Townhouses
      Designer: Harvey C. Dellinger

3057  Foxridge Apartments
      Designer: Harvey C. Dellinger

3058  Hethwood
      Designer: Harvey C. Dellinger

3059  Bruce Machinery
      Designer: Harvey C. Dellinger

3060  Broadacres Shopping Center
      Designer: Harvey C. Dellinger

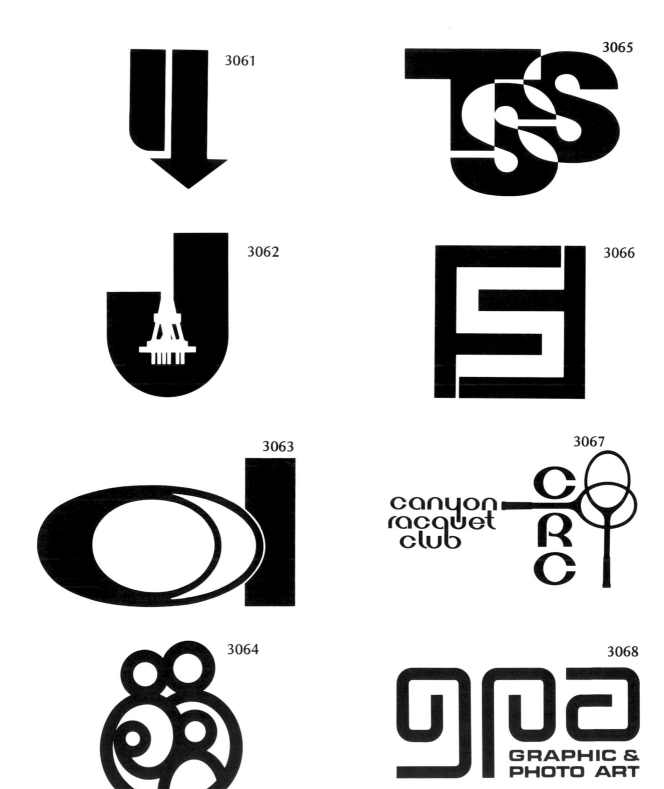

3061

3065

3062

3066

3063

3067

canyon
racquet
club

CRC

3064

3068

GRAPHIC &
PHOTO ART

 **Hershey Foods** 3069

 *Hexon* 3070

 **Allied Chemical** 3071

**TOLEDO EDISON** 3072

3061  Underground Vaults & Storage, Inc.
Designer: Ronald Muhlenbruch;
Lane & Leslie

3062  Johnson Drill Head Co.
Designer: Ronald Muhlenbruch;
Lane & Leslie

3063  Doerr Metal Products
Designer: Lane & Leslie

3064  The  Genealogical Institute
Designer: Peter J. Rabe;
Graphic & Photo Art

3065  Transportation Safety Systems
Designer: Peter J. Rabe;
Graphic & Photo Art

3066  For-Shor Company
Designer: Peter J. Rabe;
Graphic & Photo Art

3067  Canyon Racquet Club
Designer: Peter J. Rabe;
Graphic & Photo Art

3068  Graphic & Photo Art
Designer: Peter J. Rabe;
Graphic & Photo Art

3069  Hershey Foods
Hershey, Pennsylvania

3070  Hexon
Designer: Bradford-La Riviera

3071  Allied Chemical Corporation
Designer: Lubliner/Saltz, Inc.

3072  Toledo Edison
Toledo, Ohio

 3073

 3077

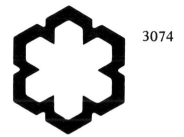 3074

 3078

 3075

 3079

Olde
English
Inn

3076

3080

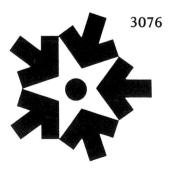

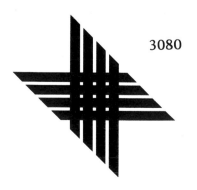

**3081**

**3082**

**3083**

**3084**

3073  Seasonal Systems Corp.
      Designer: Cottingham Advertising Design

3074  First National Bank of LaGrange
      LaGrange, Illinois

3075  Bancroft School
      Designer: George Robinson

3076  Community Rediscovery
      Designer: Bernard M. Wideroe

3077  Lyric Opera
      Designer: Bernard M. Wideroe

3078  Audiophile
      Designer: Bernard M. Wideroe

3079  Olde English Inn
      Designer: Phillips & Associates

3080  The Commercial Furnishings Group
      Designer: Wyatt L. Phillips

3081  The Benchmark Restaurant
      Designer: Phillips & Associates, Inc.

3082  Wedgewood Subdivision
      Designer: Wyatt L. Phillips

3083  The Woodlands Subdivision
      Designer: Wyatt L. Phillips

3084  Country Place Subdivision
      Designer: Wyatt L. Phillips

 3085

 3089

 3086

 3090

 3087

 3091

 3088

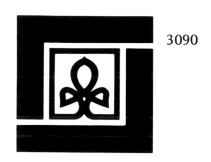 3092

 3093

 3094

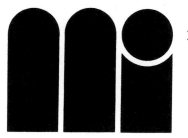 3095

 3096

3085  Mark IV Properties, Inc.
      Designer: Wyatt L. Phillips

3086  Post Properties, Inc.
      Designer: Wyatt L. Phillips

3087  Bothwell, Jenkins, Slay & Assoc., Architects
      Designer: Wyatt L. Phillips

3088  The First National Bank of Tucker
      Designer: Phillips & Associates

3089  Cox Hotel Management
      Designer: Wyatt L. Phillips

3090  Lafayette Square Apartments
      Designer: Wyatt L. Phillips

3091  Guthrie Realty Company
      Designer: Phillips & Associates, Inc.

3092  The Marketing Advisory Group
      Designer: Wyatt L. Phillips;
              The Marketing Advisory Group

3093  North National Properties
      Designer: Wyatt L. Phillips

3094  Winchester Office Park
      Designer: Phillips & Associates, Inc.

3095  Motor Inn Management
      Designer: Wyatt L. Phillips

3096  Loch Highland Subdivision
      Designer: Wyatt L. Phillips

3097

3101

northlake square

3098

3102

3099

3103

Laurelwood

3100

3104

LEHNDORFF

**Aspen Land Company**

3105

3106

3107

**SHIMANO**

3108

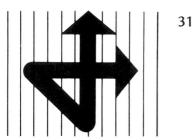 3109

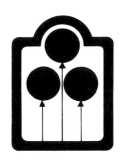 3113

 3110

 3114

 3111

 3115

3112

3116

 3117

 3118

 3120

3119

3109 Geoffrey Ladhams Associates
Designer: Monte J. Curry;
Monte J. Curry Marketing

3110 Plasmold, Inc.
Designer: Monte J. Curry

3111 Providence Properties, Inc.
Designer: Monte J. Curry

3112 Decorative Components Division,
Polysar Plastics, Inc.
Designer: Elaine M. Lyerly;
Monte J. Curry Marketing

3113 River Hills Plantation (special celebration)
Designer: Elaine M. Lyerly;
Monte J. Curry Marketing

3114 Signseal
Designer: Elaine M. Lyerly;
Monte J. Curry Marketing

3115 Repro/Graphics
Designer: Elaine M. Lyerly;
Monte J. Curry Marketing

3116 Media-Concepts, Inc.
Designer: Monte J. Curry

3117 Apartment Locator Service
Designer: Monte J. Curry

3118 The Cove Condominium
Designer: Elaine M. Lyerly
Monte J. Curry Marketing

3119 Street Development Company
Designer: Monte J. Curry

3120 D.C. Turner Construction Co.
Designer: Monte J. Curry

 3121

 3125

 3122

 3126

 3123

 3127

 3124

 3128

3129

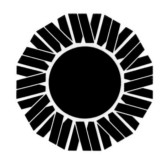

3130

3131

3132

3121 Modern Management, Inc.
Designer: Elaine M. Lyerly;
Monte J. Curry Marketing

3122 The Lodge
Designer: Elaine M. Lyerly;
Monte J. Curry Marketing

3123 Pat Wagner Communications
Designer: Monte J. Curry

3124 Mimosa Hills Golf Club
Designer: Elaine M. Lyerly;
Monte J. Curry Marketing

3125 Providence Square Racquet Club
Designer: Monte J. Curry

3126 Gordon Gutke Advertising Art
Designer: Gordon Gutke Advertising Art

3127 Travel Desk (travel agency)
Designer: Gordon Gutke Advertising Art

3128 Century Incentives
Designer: Gordon Gutke Advertising Art

3129 Fabricators Inc.
Designer: Gordon Gutke Advertising Art

3130 Washington County (proposed)
Designer: Gordon Gutke Advertising Art

3131 J. Plush Brush (beauty parlor)
Designer: Gordon Gutke Advertising Art

3132 Insta-Just (hydraulic chair)
Designer: Gordon Gutke Advertising Art

 3133

 3137

 3134

 3138

 3135

 3139

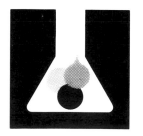 3136

 3140

3141

3142

3143

3144

3133 Krengel Machine Company, Inc.
Designer: Gordon Gutke Advertising Art

3134 C and L Business Systems
Designer: Gordon Gutke Advertising Art

3135 Brown Equipment Co.
Designer: Gordon Gutke Advertising Art

3136 Ute Research Laboratories
Designer: Gordon Gutke Advertising Art

3137 Gateway Finance Company
Designer: Gordon Gutke Advertising Art

3138 Concept Industries Corporation
Designer: Gordon Gutke Advertising Art

3139 Trevarrow, Inc.
Designer: Al Weston

3140 Miramos
Designer: Rolf H. Paul Graphics

3141 West Nebraska General Hospital
Designer: Rolf H. Paul Graphics

3142 Black Hawk Enterprises
Designer: Rolf H. Paul Graphics

3143 The Market Place
Designer: Rolf H. Paul Graphics

3144 American Lightbulb Supply Co.
Designer: Rolf H. Paul Graphics

 3145

 3149

 3146

 3150

 3147

 3151

 3148

 3152

 3153

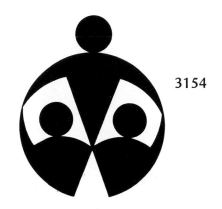 3154

 3155

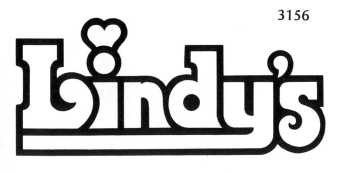 3156

3145  Bulldog Enterprises
      Designer: Rolf H. Paul Graphics

3146  Wells Inc.
      Designer: Rolf H. Paul Graphics

3147  Monticore
      Designer: Rolf H. Paul Graphics

3148  Transportation Adv. Associates
      Designer: Mike Miller; Graphic Art Services

3149  Roy Clark
      Designer: Mike Miller; Graphic Art Services

3150  Alpine Pest Control
      Designer: Mike Miller; Graphic Art Services

3151  Mom Productions
      Designer: Mike Miller; Graphic Art Services

3152  Cabaret Productions
      Designer: Mike Miller; Graphic Art Services

3153  Joanne Halsey
      Designer: John Dykema; Graphic Art Services

3154  Institute of Pastoral Counseling
      Designer: Herb Hansen; Graphic Art Services

3155  Royal Foods
      Designer: Mike Miller; Graphic Arts Services

3156  Lindy's — Flamingo Hotel
      Designer: Mike Miller; Graphic Art Services

 3157

 3161

 3158

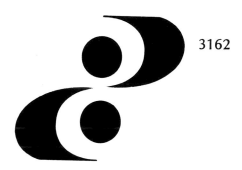 3162

 3159

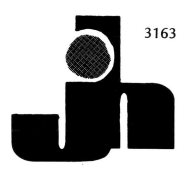 3163

 3160

 3164

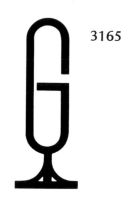

3165

3166

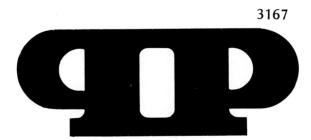

3167

3168

3157   JCS Bench Company
Designer: Mike Miller; Graphic Art Services

3158   Five Companies Inc.
Designer: Mike Miller; Graphic Art Services

3159   Landmark Hotel
Designer: Mike Miller; Graphic Art Services

3160   Cambridge Racquet Club
Designer: Mike Miller; Graphic Art Services

3161   Family Doctors of Nevada
Designer: Mike Miller; Graphic Art Services

3162   KLAS-TV 8
Designer: Mike Miller; Graphic Art Services

3163   Jim Halsey Company
Designer: Mike Miller; Graphic Art Services

3164   Joe Peterson Interiors
Designer: Mike Miller; Graphic Art Services

3165   Gentry Sound
Designer: Herb Hansen; Graphic Art Services

3166   B & G International
Designer: Mike Miller; Graphic Art Services

3167   Pagama Productions
Designer: Mike Miller; Graphic Art Services

3168   Flamingo Hotel
Designer: Mike Miller; Graphic Art Services

 3169

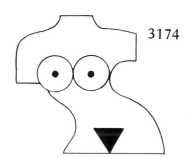 3173

 3170

 3174

 3171

 3174

 3172

 3176

3177

3178

3179

3180

3169  Home Savings and Loan Association
      Designer: Lawrence E. Pelini

3170  Kewanee National Bank
      Designer: Lawrence E. Pelini

3171  Lawrence E. Pelini Studio Ltd.
      Designer: Lawrence E. Pelini

3172  Association for Modern Banking in Illinois
      Designer: Lawrence E. Pelini

3173  Heart of Illinois Beef Association
      Designer: Lawrence E. Pelini

3174  Brenda/Artists Model
      Designer: Lawrence E. Pelini

3175  Westchester Library System
      White Plains, New York

3176  First Empire Bank — New York
      Designer: Paul Sandhaus Associates

3177  O'Connor Realty
      Designer: Funk Advertising Company

3178  Taylor Building Products
      Designer: Kevin Tolman; Artra Associates

3179  Brand Names Foundation, Inc.
      Designer: Paul Hansbursin

3180  Mountain House
      Oregon Freeze Dry Foods, Inc.
      Albany, Oregon

3181

3182

3183

3184

3185

3186

3187

bell

3188

3189

3190

3191

3192

3181 Tempo Leasing Corp.
Designer: Douglas C. Granger;
Leslie Advertising

3182 Recordplate Company, Inc.
Designer: James M. Walker

3183 American Pioneer Center
Designer: Alan Leitstein

3184 "The Links" Golf Country Club
Designer: Alan Leitstein

3185 Alan Stuart Leitstein
Designer: Alan Leitstein

3186 Florida Living Center
Designer: Alan Leitstein

3187 Bell Mortgage Corporation
Designer: Alan Leitstein

3188 C.E. Industries Inc.
Designer: Alan Leitstein

3189 PSI Industries
Designer: William W. Chapman;
CPS Communications

3190 Plico Products
Designer: William W. Chapman;
CPS Communications

3191 Texas Plasticote Inc.
Designer: William W. Chapman/
Robert Giaimo; CPS
Communications

3192 NRG Incorporated
Designer: Kidder Axelson
& Associates, Inc.

 3193

 3197

 3194

 3198

**The
Communications
Board** 3195

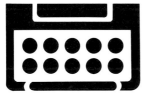

3199

3196

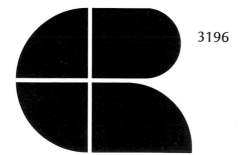

 3200

3201

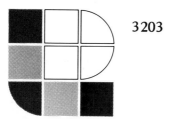

3202

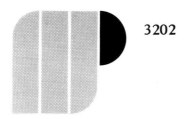

3203

3204

3193  Devi Productions, Inc.
      Designer: Mike Quon

3194  Mike Quon Graphic Design
      Designer: Mike Quon

3195  The Communications Board
      Designer: Mike Quon

3196  Capital Planning Resources
      Designer: Mike Quon

3197  Executive Systems Planning
      Designer: Mike Quon

3198  The Fifth Season
      Designer: Mike Quon

3199  Jeffrey Hirsch, Inc.
      Designer: Mike Quon

3200  Capital Liquidity, Inc.
      Designer: Mike Quon

3201  Chan Plumbing
      Designer: Mike Quon

3202  Mission Mobile Products, Inc.
      Designer: Mike Quon

3203  Leisure Design, Inc.
      Designer: Mike Quon

3204  Beverly Hills Travel
      Designer: Mike Quon

 3205

 3209

 3206

 3210

 3207

 3211

 3208

 3212

 3213

 3214

 Dan River®

 3215

 3216

3205  Western Bass Anglers Association
      Designer: Mike Quon

3206  Outagamie Democtars
      Designer: Pat Taylor

3207  Kimberly-Clark Corp. (Erasable Bond)
      Designer: Pat Taylor

3208  Gerry Kanode
      Designer: Pat Taylor

3209  Urban Land Perspectives Inc.
      Designer: Pat Taylor

3210  TYO Publishing Co.
      Designer: Pat Taylor

3211  Dana Research Inc.
      Designer: Pat Taylor

3212  Combined Communications Corporation
      Designer: Barry Wickliffe

3212  The Sherwin-Williams Company
      Designer: F. Eugene Smith Associates

3214  Dan River Inc.
      Designer: Sandgren & Murtha, Inc.

3215  Xeroil Corporation
      Designer: Don A. Primi; Industrial Advertising
            Associates, Inc.

3216  Flightline
      Designer: Milton Chun

3217

3221

3218

3222

3219

3223

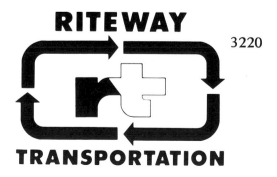
3220

3224

3225

3226

3227

3217 Mique Quenzer Directions Inc.
Designer: Milton Chun

3218 Diversified Graphic Impressions
Designer: Frank A. Gutierrez

3219 Pro-Motions
Designer: Frank A. Gutierrez

3220 Riteway Transportation
Designer: Frank A. Gutierrez

3221 Alec Litho
Designer: Frank A. Gutierrez

3222 Cano Electric
Designer: Frank A. Gutierrez

3223 Z.A.C. Charro Association (Mexican Rodeo)
Designer: Frank A. Gutierrez

3224 Spanish-American Institute
Designer: Frank A. Gutierrez

3225 Pat McCormick Enterprises
Designer: Frank A. Gutierrez

3226 College of Agriculture and Life Sciences Fund
Designer: James K. Estes

3227 Bank of New Hampshire N.A.
Manchester, New Hampshire

3228 William Seifert
Designer: William Seifert

3228

William Seifert
graphic design photography
350 East 52nd street
apt. 12-K
New York New York 10022

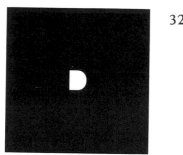 3229

 3233

 3220

 3234

 3231

 3235

 3232

 3236

3237

3238

3239

3240

3229 The Drake Office
Designer: Melville M. Drake

3230 Pro-Mote, Inc.
Designer: Melville M. Drake

3231 Republic Savings & Loan
Designer: Melville M. Drake

3232 New Process Corporation
Designer: Melville M. Drake

3233 Brookfield Hills
Designer: Melville M. Drake

3234 Logan & Associates
Designer: Melville M. Drake

3235 Wilson, Haas & Associates, Inc.
Designer: Melville M. Drake

3236 Communications for Hospitals, Inc.
Designer: Richard Morgado Designer

3237 Crotched Mountain
Designer: Richard Morgado Designer

3238 Glen Terrace Nurseries
Designer: Anita Soos

3239 Warsaw Agency
Designer: Anita Soos

3240 Office Interiors, Inc.
Designer: Anita Soos

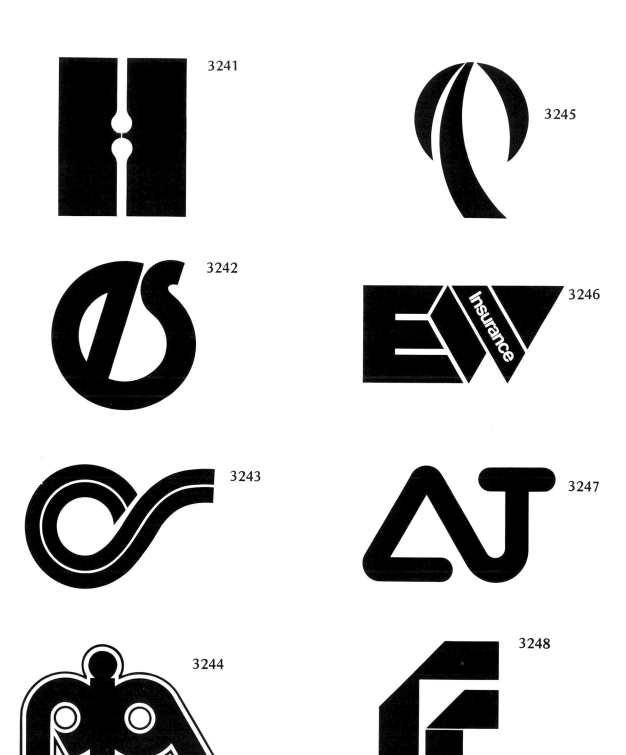

3241

3245

3242

3246

Insurance

3243

3247

3244

3248

**3249**

Career Directions

3250

3251

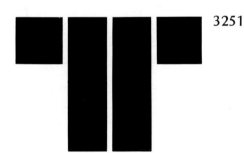

3252

3241  Heinsz Insurance Agency, Inc.
Designer: Anita Soos

3242  Edward J. Smith Assocs./Advertising
Designer: Anita Soos

3243  Carl Scholl Insurance
Designer: Anita Soos

3244  Potter Insurance Agency
Designer: Anita Soos

3245  Palm Beach Insurance Central, Inc.
Designer: Anita Soos

3246  Emery-Webb, Inc.
Designer: Anita Soos

3247  Arnold Jones Insurance Agency
Designer: Anita Soos

3248  Fulmer & Company
Designer: Anita Soos

3249  Aetna Life & Casualty
Designer: Anita Soos

3250  Larson, Raikko & Weaver, Inc.
Designer: Anita Soos

3251  Tubertini-Hillhouse Insurance Agency, Inc.
Designer: Anita Soos

3252  Nussear Insurance Agency, Inc.
Designer: Anita Soos

3253

3257

small
world

3254

3258

3255

3259

OAKCREST

3256

3260

TIERRA CAVO

3261

3262

3253 Crowell C. Hall
Designer: Anita Soos

3254 Small World Childrens Day School
Designer: Jess Gruel; Larson-Bateman, Inc.

3255 Quadrant Development Corp.
Designer: Jess Gruel; Larson-Bateman, Inc.

3256 Santa Barbara Photo Engravers
Designer: Jess Gruel; Larson-Bateman, Inc.

3257 Bank of Montecito
Designer: Jess Gruel; Larson-Bateman, Inc.

3258 Jolly Tiger Restaurants
Designer: Jess Gruel; Larson-Bateman, Inc.

3259 Oakcrest
Designer: Jess Gruel; Larson-Bateman, Inc.

3260 Tierra Cavo
Designer: Jess Gruel; Larson-Bateman, Inc.

3261 Michael Towbes Construction Co.
Designer: Jess Gruel; Larson-Bateman, Inc.

3262 Boulder Creek Golf & Country Club
Designer: Jess Gruel; Larson-Bateman, Inc.

3263 Calvary Presbyterian Church
Designer: Everett Forbes

3264 Vanguard Advertising, Inc.
Designer: Everett Forbes

3263

CALVARY
PRESBYTERIAN
CHURCH

3264

3265

3269

3266

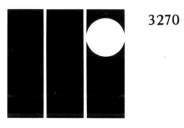

3270

3267

3271

3268

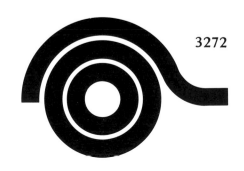

3272

 3273

 3274

3265  Bayside Hospital
      Designer: Everett Forbes

3266  The Colonies
      Designer: Everett Forbes

3267  Dorey Electrical Contractors
      Designer: Everett Forbes

3268  Yancey Brothers Co.
      Designer: Robert C. Manning

3269  Arkansas Society of Communication Arts
      Designer: Tom Henton

3270  Markham Inn Hotel
      Designer: Tom Henton

3271  Capital Club
      Designer: Tom Henton

 3275

3272  Roberts Brothers Tire Service
      Designer: Tom Henton

3273  Varco-Pruden, Inc.
      Designer: Tom Henton

3274  Faulkner-Watkins & Assocs.
      Designer: Tom Henton

3275  Pacesetter Corporation
      Designer: Tom Henton

 3276

3276  AFCO Metals, Inc.
      Designer: Tom Henton

 3277

 3281

 3278

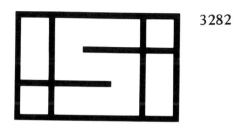 3282

 3279

 3283

 3280

3284

**Citibank**

*The Clara Laughlin Travel Services Inc.*

3285

*Money Shop*

3286

SALVATION

3287

Scovill

3288

 3289

 3293

 3290

 3294

 3291

 3295

3292

 3296

# PUBLICITY/PUBLIC RELATIONS

3298

PALMBROOK
COUNTRY CLUB

3299

secluded *acres

3300

Chaparral Rancheros

3289 Rainbow Slump Block Co.
Designer: Marie Martel

3290 Distinctive Designs
Designer: Marie Martel

3291 Professional Corporation Portfolios
Designer: Marie Martel

3292 National Speakers Association
Designer: Marie Martel

3293 Estrella Ranch
Designer: Marie Martel

3294 Marina City Club
Designer: Marie Martel

3295 Aid to Zoo Horse Show
Designer: Marie Martel

3296 Sickles Sales & Service
Designer: Marie Martel

3297 Maxine Olmsted Publicity
Designer: Marie Martel

3298 Palmbrook Country Club
Designer: Marie Martel

3299 Secluded Acres
Designer: Marie Martel

3300 Chaparral Rancheros
Designer: Marie Martel

 3301

 3305

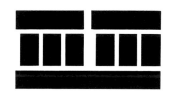 3302

 3306

 3303

 3307

 3304

 3308

**3309**

**3310**

**3311**

**3312**

3301 The Starr Company
Designer: Marie Martel

3302 Marie Martel
Designer: Marie Martel

3303 Dew Park
Designer: Marie Martel

3304 Dew Guard
Designer: Marie Martel

3305 Everson Electric Company
Designer: Marie Martel

3306 Frank Walls/Property Consultants
Designer: Marie Martel

3307 Richter & Tate Insurance Company
Designer: Marie Martel

3308 International Venture Research
Designer: Marie Martel

3309 Olive Square
Designer: Marie Martel

3310 Wild West Marketing
Designer: Marie Martel

3311 Heddy's House of Wigs
Designer: Marie Martel

3312 Del Webb's Sun City
Designer: Marie Martel & Dick Sorel

 3313

 3317

 3314

Prudential Plaza

 3318

 3315

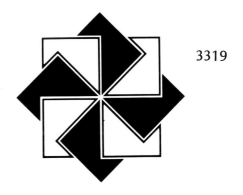 3319

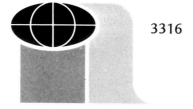 3316

 3320

L.C. Jacobson

**3321**

**3322**

**3323**

WATER-PEDS

**3324**

3313  Jacobson Diversified
     Designer: Marie Martel

3314  Prudential Plaza
     Designer: Marie Martel

3315  La Ronde Centre
     Designer: Marie Martel

3316  International Acceptance Co.
     Designer: Marie Martel

3317  Market Impact, Inc.
     Designer: Marie Martel

3318  Irving Jennings & Associates
     Designer: Marie Martel

3319  Diversified Personal Services
     Designer: Marie Martel

3320  L.C. Jacobson
     Designer: Marie Martel

3321  Interpac Intermountain, Inc..
     Designer: Marie Martel

3322  Imperial Lithographers, Inc.
     Designer: Marie Martel

3323  Water-Peds
     Designer: Marie Martel

3324  Mountain Valley Transportation Co.
     Designer: Marie Martel

 3325

 3329

 3326

romar
inc.

 3330

 3327

 3331

Cara Nova

 3328

 3332

3333

3334

3335

3336

3325  Sunland Paper Company
      Designer: Marie Martel

3326  Romar, Inc.
      Designer: Marie Martel

3327  R.M. Bowlsby & Associates
      Designer: Marie Martel

3328  Valley Beautiful Citizens Council, Inc.
      Designer: Marie Martel

3329  Val Moritz
      Designer: Marie Martel

3330  R.M. Wartes
      Designer: Marie Martel

3331  Cara Nova, Inc.
      Designer: Marie Martel

3332  Cash, Sullivan & Cross
      Designer: Marie Martel

3333  Del Webb's Towne House
      Designer: Marie Martel

3334  Plaza Liquors
      Designer: Marie Martel

3335  Los Angeles Music & Art School
      Designer: Frank A. Gutierrez

3336  Fair Lawn Industries, Inc.
      Designer: David Leigh

 3337

 3341

 3338

 3342

 3343

 3339

 3340

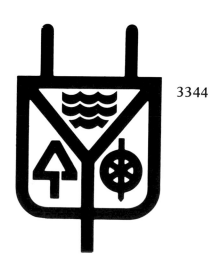 3344

 3345

 3346

 3347

 3348

3349

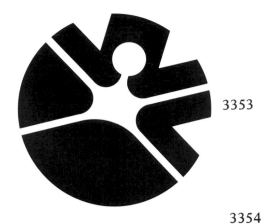
3353

3350

3354

3351

3355

**ESMARK** 3352

3356

3357

3358

3359

3349 Mariner's Resort Inn
     Designer: Everett Forbes

3350 Chewning, Hoggard, Adkins, Engineers
     Designer: Everett Forbes

3351 Lloyd Chester Associates
     Designer: Mike Quon

3352 Esmark, Inc.
     Designer: Anspach, Grossman Inc.

3353 University of Rochester, Student Activities
       Center
     Designer: Stephen Reynolds

3354 Enterprise Press
     Designer: Stephen Reynolds

3355 SMH-Art Council
     Designer: Stephen Reynolds

3356 Morgan Yacht Corporation
     Designer: Bradley Yeager;
       Bradley Yeager & Associates, Inc.

3357 Public Information, Inc.
     Designer: Joe Dill; Bradley Yeager & Associates

3358 Easton Realty
     Designer: Gary Brown;
       Bradley Yeager & Associates, Inc.

3359 Oak Lake Park
     Designer: Gary Brown;
       Bradley Yeager & Associates, Inc.

3360

3364

3361

3365

3362

3363

3366

 3367

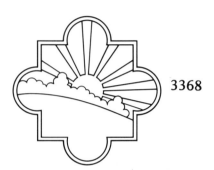 3368

 3369

3360 Mariner Village
Designer: Joe Dill; Bradley Yeager & Associates

3361 Carl Kuttler
Designer: Gary Brown
Bradley Yeager & Associates, Inc.

3362 Imperial Palms Village
Designer: Joe Dill; Bradley Yeager & Associates

3363 Bruce Little Co., Plumbing
Designer: Joe Dill; Bradley Yeager & Associates

3364 Jerger & Sons, Inc.
Designer: Gary Brown;
Bradley Yeager & Associates, Inc.

3365 Ellis First National Bank
Designer: Gary Brown;
Bradley Yeager & Associates, Inc.

3366 Winding Creek
Designer: Gary Brown;
Bradley Yeager & Associates, Inc.

3367 Rodgers & Associates
Designer: Marvin L. Joseph

3368 Serinada Country Estates
Designer: Joseph Advertising Design

3369 Dave Shanks
Designer: Marvin L. Joseph

3370 Austin Meters Inc.
Designer: Joseph Advertising Design

 3370

3371

 PAL-CHEM INDUSTRIES, INC.

3375

3372

3373

3376

3374

CRAFTS & CULTURE

 **3377**

 **3378**

 **3379**

 **3380**

3371 Pal-Chem Industries, Inc.
Designer: Joseph Advertising Design

3372 Babcock Co.
Designer: Marvin L. Joseph

3373 Knight, Walsh & Associates, Inc.
Designer: Kerry Walsh; Knight, Walsh & Assocs.

3374 Crafts & Culture
Designer: Knight, Walsh & Associates

3375 College of the Ozarks
Designer: Knight, Walsh & Associates

3376 Tonkawa High School, Class of 64 Reunion
Designer: Knight, Walsh & Associates

3377 Peoples Gas Co.
Designer: Arnold La Bahn, Robert Sychowski

3378 R. K. P. Associates
Designer: Jonathan Pieslak

3379 Jonathan Pieslak
Designer: Jonathan Pieslak

3380 Rae Real Estate and Management Co.
Designer: Jonathan Pieslak

3381

LECTURES/SEMINARS/BROADCASTING

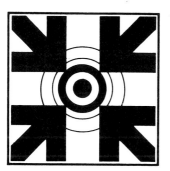

3382

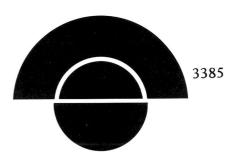

3385

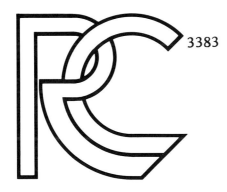

3383

3386

3384

3387

**3388**

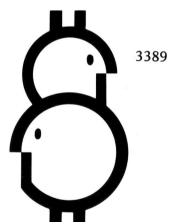

**3389**

**3390**

3381  Robert Anthony Presentations
Designer Michael Kowalczyk

3382  New England Site Locators
Designer: Michael Kowalczyk

3383  Riccardo Caine Photography
Designer: Michael Kowalczyk

3384  Edward A. Saunders
Designer: Edward A. Saunders

3385  Halawa Grand Condominium
Designer: Edward A. Saunders

3386  "Kekuaananui" Hawaii Big Sisters, Inc.
Designer: Edward A. Saunders

3387  Hawaiian Mortgage Co., Inc.
Designer: Edward A. Saunders

3388  Hawaiian Banana Company
Designer: Edward A. Saunders

3389  Reliable Finance Inc.
Designer: Ray Ainsworth

3390  Reliable Finance Inc.
Designer: Ray Ainsworth

3391

3394

3392

3395

3393

**WABE**
**FM90.1**

3396

**3397**

**3398**

Barwick
Banking
Company

**3399**

**3400**

CHINESE AMERICAN INSTITUTE

3391  Butterfield National Bank
Designer: Steve Skaggs

3392  Southern National Bank
Designer: Steve Skaggs

3393  Public Broadcasting Atlanta
Designer: Steve Skaggs

3394  Courier Checks (nursery, child care)
Designer: Steve Skaggs

3395  Courier Checks (youth organization)
Designer: Steve Skaggs

3396  Courier Checks (smoke shop)
Designer: Steve Skaggs

3397  Camden State Bank
Designer: Steve Skaggs

3398  Barwick Banking Company
Designer: Steve Skaggs

3399  Bank of Montecito
Designer: Steve Skaggs

3400  Chinese-American Institute
Designer: Steve Skaggs/Mei Wu

WETV30

3401

3404

3405

3402

3403

BECA

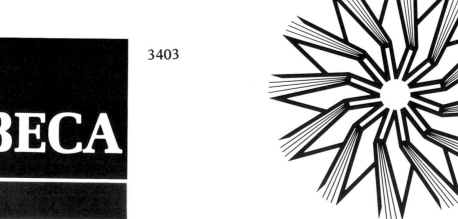

3406

3407

3408

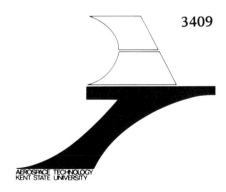

3409

3410

3411

SUPERIOR
DESIGN CO., INC.

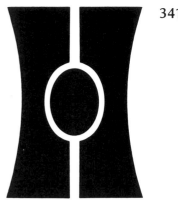

3415

3412

car
care
council

3413

3416

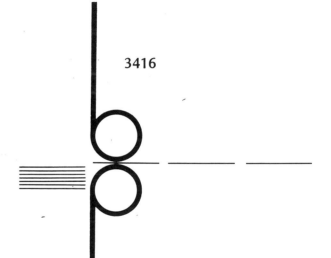

3414

GRAFIX

3417

3418

3419

3420

3411  Superior Design, Inc.
      Designer: Paul S. Weiser

3412  Car Care Council
      Dearborn, Michigan

3413  Sugarcreek Concepts
      Designer: Reginald K. Litten

3414  Reg Litten Grafix
      Designer: Reginald K. Litten

3415  The Hewitt Soap Co., Inc.
      Designer: Reginald K. Litten

3416  Bramkamp Printing Co., Inc.
      Designer: Reginald K. Litten

3417  Perfection Tool & Mold Corporation
      Designer: Reginald K. Litten

3418  Kickham Boiler and Engineering, Inc.
      Designer: Mel Zimmerman

3419  The Graphic Statement
      Designer: Michael Pacey/Supergraphics

3420  The Sleeping Bird (antique shop)
      Designer: Michael Pacey/Supergraphics

3421

3425

3422

3426

3423

3427

3424

3428

3429

3430

3431

3432

# THE JEFFERSON SQUARE

3421  YWCA
    Designer: J. David Suggs

3422  Flexi Wall Corporation
    Designer: J. David Suggs

3423  Project Haiti
    Designer: J. David Suggs

3424  South Carolina Department of
        Parks, Recreation and Tourism
    Designer: J. David Suggs

3425  South Carolina Tricentennial Celebration
    Designer: J. David Suggs

3426  Columbia Drug Response Celebration
    Designer: J. David Suggs

3427  South Carolina Department of Mental Health
    Designer: J. David Suggs

3428  Standard Corporation and the
        Standard Warehouse Company
    Designer: J. David Suggs

3429  South Carolina Department of Social Services
    Designer: J. David Suggs

3430  South Carolina Baptist Campus Ministries
    Designer: J. David Suggs

3431  Pentagon Corporation
    Designer: J. David Suggs

3432  The Jefferson Square Theatre
    Designer: J. David Suggs

3433

3437

3438

3434

3435

3439

3436

3440

3441

3442

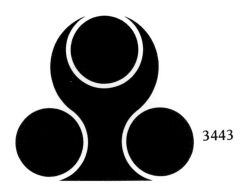

3443

3444

3433 Greater Carolinas Corporation
Designer: J. David Suggs

3434 Alston Wilkes Society
Designer: J. David Suggs

3435 Fox Music House
Designer: J. David Suggs

3436 Contact Help
Designer: J. David Suggs

3437 Carolina Coliseum
Designer: J. David Suggs

3438 Eve's Apple Incorporated
Designer: J. David Suggs

3439 Columbia Bible College
Designer: J. David Suggs

3440 First Federal Savings & Loan Association
Designer: J. David Suggs

3441 Greater Myrtle Beach Chamber of Commerce
Designer: J. David Suggs

3442 Burriss Construction Co.
Designer: J. David Suggs

3443 South Carolina Governors
      Beautification and Improvement Board
Designer: J. David Suggs

3444 Columbia Urban Service Center
Designer: J. David Suggs

 3445

 3449

 3446

Rebel 3450

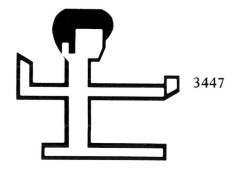 3447

 3451

 3448

 3452

**3453**

3445  Chatham Steel Corporation
Designer: J. David Suggs

3446  Bass Enterprises
Designer: J. David Suggs

3447  Bethleham Community Center
Designer: J. David Suggs

3448  Universal Business Machines Inc.
Designer: J. David Suggs

3449  Dutch Center
Designer: J. David Suggs

3450  Rebel Boat Trailers
Designer: J. David Suggs

3451  South Carolina Commission on
Water Resources
Designer: J. David Suggs

3452  South Carolina Council for Human Rights
Designer: J. David Suggs

3453  Sound Investment
Designer: Michael Pacey/Supergraphics

 3454

GreenMark
INCORPORATED

 3458

 3455

 3459

watts
POOL COMPANY

 3456

HOUSTON ADVERTISING CLUB

 3460

 3457

 3461

**3462**

3454  GreenMark Incorporated
       Designer: Baxter + Korge

3455  American Society for Oceanography
       Designer: Baxter + Korge

3456  Houston Advertising Club
       Designer: Baxter + Korge

3457  Houston National Bank
       Designer: Baxter + Korge

3458  Lincoln Consolidated, Inc.
       Designer: Baxter + Korge

3459  Watts Pool Company
       Designer: Baxter + Korge

3460  Gulf Atlantic
       Designer: Baxter + Korge

3461  Plaza del Oro Corporation
       Designer: Baxter + Korge

3462  One Shell Plaza
       Designer: Baxter + Korge

3463

3465

USAA

3466

3467

3468

3464

**Transsco Companies Inc.** 3469

3470

3471

3472

3463  Kamel's World of Travel, Inc.
      Designer: Baxter + Korge

3464  Mill House Restaurant, Inc.
      Designer: Baxter + Korge

3465  United Services Automobile Association
      Designer: Baxter + Korge

3466  Russo Financial Corporation
      Designer: Baxter + Korge

3467  Associated Credit Bureaus, Inc.
      Designer: Baxter + Korge

3468  Greenway Bank & Trust
      Designer: Baxter + Korge

3469  Transco Companies, Inc.
      Designer: Baxter + Korge

3470  Anderson Clayton
      Designer: Baxter + Korge

3471  Continex
      Designer: Baxter + Korge

3472  Mama Rizzo's
      Designer: Baxter + Korge

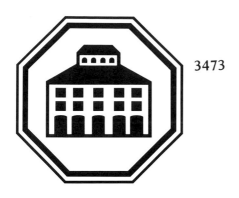 3473

 3477

 3474

 3478

 3473

 3479

 3476

 3480

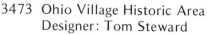

3473 Ohio Village Historic Area
Designer: Tom Steward

3474 Southeastern Michigan
Transportation Authority
Designer: Jac Purdon

3475 Southeastern Michigan
Transportation Authority
Designer: Jac Purdon

3476 Community Theatre Assn. of Michigan
Designer: Jac Purdon

3477 Non Smokers Inc.
Designer: Jac Purdon

3478 The Bikery
Designer: Donald Mclean;
George N. Sepetys & Associates

3479 Homewood Building Company
Designer: William Davis;
George N. Sepetys & Associates

3480 Rust-Shield
Designer: William Davis;
George N. Sepetys & Associates

3481 Corporate & Association Meeting Services, Inc.
Designer: Thomas Winberry;
George N. Sepetys & Associates

3482 G & S Associates, Inc.
Designer: Thomas Winberry
George N. Sepetys & Associates

3483 Nylok-Detroit
Designer: Michael Cromwell;
George N. Sepetys & Associates

3484 United Skiers Service
Designer: Michael Cromwell;
George N. Sepetys & Associates

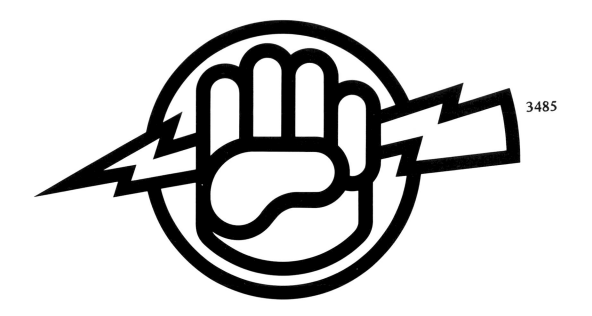

3485

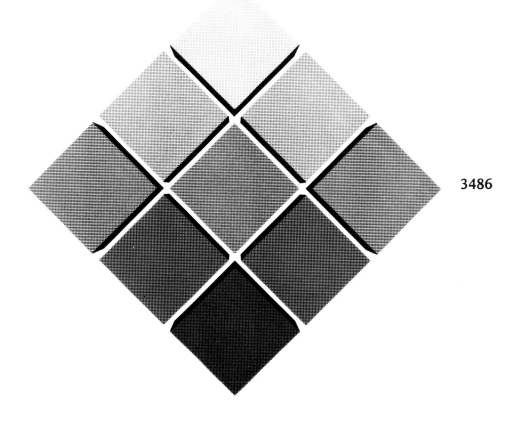

3486

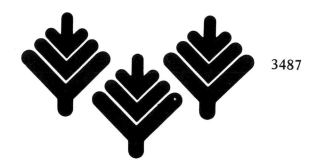 3487

 3488

 3489

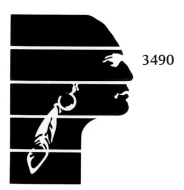 3490

3485  Electrical Contractors Association
      Designer: Donald Mclean;
          George N. Sepetys & Associates

3486  Bruce Crockford, Architect
      Designer: Michael Cromell;
          George N. Sepetys & Associates

3487  Korson's Tree Farms
      Designer: Donald Mclean;
          George N. Sepetys & Associates

3488  Sound-Wave Systems, Inc.
      Designer: Donald Mclean;
          George N. Sepetys & Associates

3489  Travel Center Ski Tours
      Designer: William Davis;
          George N. Sepetys & Associates

3490  Pontiac Stadium Building Authority
      Designer: William Davis;
          George N. Sepetys & Associates

3491

3495

3492

3496

3493

3497

3494

3498

3499

3500

3501

3502

3491 Office Concepts
Designer: William Davis;
George N. Sepetys & Associates

3492 Detroit Suburban Network
Designer: William Davis;
George N. Sepetys & Associates

3493 Glen Flora Country Club
Designer: William Davis;
George N. Sepetys & Associates

3494 The Bill Sandy Co.
Designer: George Sepetys;
George N. Sepetys & Associates

3495 Michigan Stags
Designer: Donald Mclean;
George N. Sepetys & Associates

3496 Somerset Inn
Designer: William Davis;
George N. Sepetys & Associates

3497 J.A. Citrin Sons Company
Designer: William Davis;
George N. Sepetys & Associates

3498 Woodlands
Designer: William Davis;
George N. Sepetys & Associates

3499 The Communication Counsel of America
Designer: Don Weller

3500 Mott Media (for series of books)
Designer: Don Weller

3501 Galleon Productions
Designer: Don Weller/Mark Erickson

3502 Antique Arcade of Beverly Hills
Designer: Don Weller/Bob Maile

 3503

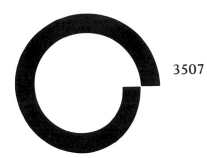 3507

 3504

 3508

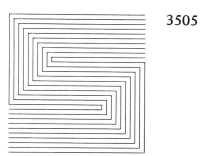 3505

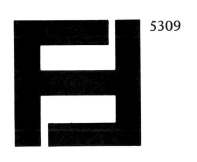 5309

 3506

 3510

Geotek incorporated

# HAYLOFT TOYS, CRAFTS + COUNTRY CLOTHES 3511

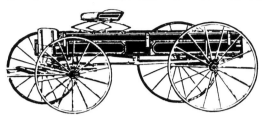

**3512**

**3513**

HFRC

**3514**

TWeeD

3503 Sports Riders Assn. of Colorado
Designer: Mark Mock

3504 V'Soske
Designer: David Bates

3505 Henry K. Szwarce, Architect
Designer: e. christopher klumb

3506 Benedictine Monks Weston Priory
Designer: e. christopher klumb

3507 Anthony Cipriano Sculpture Studio & Gallery
Designer: e. christopher klumb

3508 Vicovaro Foundation Inc.
Designer: e. christopher klumb

3509 Bruce Fowle/Architect
Designer: e. christopher klumb

3510 Geotek Incorporated
Designer: e. christopher klumb

3511 Hayloft
Designer: e. christopher klumb

3512 IM International
Designer: e. christopher klumb

3513 AIA, Health Facilities Resource Center
Designer: e. christopher klumb

3514 The Tweed Shops
Designer: e. christopher klumb

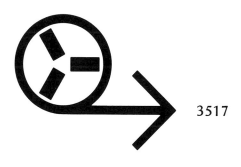 3515

 3519

 3516

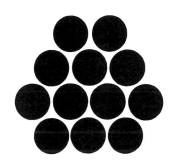 3520

 3521

3517

 3518

 3522

# S. BERKOWITZ + ASSOCIATES 3523

3524

3525

3526

3527

3528

3529

3530

3531

3532

3533

3534

**3535**

**3536**

**3537**

**3538**

3527 Dallas Museum of Fine Arts
Designer: Crawford Dunn; RYA Graphics, Inc.

3528 Faxon Incorporated
Designer: Crawford Dunn; RYA Graphics, Inc.

3529 The Texas Group
Designer: Crawford Dunn; RYA Graphics, Inc.

3530 WBAP-AM/FM
Designer: Crawford Dunn; RYA Graphics, Inc.

3531 Sands Measurement Corporation
Designer: Crawford Dunn; RYA Graphics, Inc.

3532 North Texas State University
Designer: Crawford Dunn; RYA Graphics, Inc.

3533 Brookhollow Business Park
Designer: Crawford Dunn; RYA Graphics, Inc.

3534 Northlake College
Designer: Crawford Dunn; RYA Graphics, Inc.

3535 Vision Center
Designer: Crawford Dunn; RYA Graphics, Inc.

3536 Lamm-Frates Company
Designer: Crawford Dunn; RYA Graphics, Inc.

3537 Eastland Bank
Designer: Crawford Dunn; RYA Graphics, Inc.

3538 Zale Corporation
Designer: Crawford Dunn/Larry Roberts

 3539

 3540

 3541

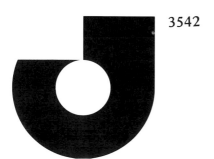 3542

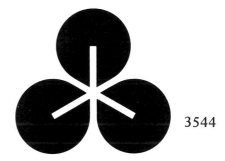 3543

 3544

 3545

3546

 3547

 3548

 3549

SOUTHERN
METHODIST
UNIVERSITY
DIVISION
OF
MUSIC

3539  Westchase Corporation
      Designer: Crawford Dunn, RYA Graphics, Inc..

3540  Wilhide Interiors
      Designer: Crawford Dunn; RYA Graphics, Inc.

3541  First National Bank of Abilene
      Designer: Crawford Dunn; RYA Graphics, Inc.

3542  Grady Jordan & Company
      Designer: Crawford Dunn; RYA Graphics, Inc.

3543  Town Center at Chevy Chase
      Designer: Crawford Dunn; RYA Graphics, Inc.

3544  Envirodynamics Incorporated
      Designer: Crawford Dunn; RYA Graphics, Inc.

3545  Broadnax Printing Company
      Designer: Crawford Dunn: RYA Graphics, Inc.

3546  Guardian Savings
      Designer: Crawford Dunn; RYA Graphics, Inc.

3547  Campbell Centre
      Designer: Crawford Dunn; RYA Graphics, Inc.

3548  Jokari U.S. Inc.
      Designer: Crawford Dunn/Harve Hugman

3549  Southern Methodist University
      Designer: Crawford Dunn; RYA Graphics, Inc.

3550  Henry C. Beck Company
      Designer: Crawford Dunn; RYA Graphics, Inc.

 3550

3551

3555

3552

3556

**Streams
and
Valleys** 3553

3557

3558
3554

 3559

 3560

3561

3562

3551 Fisher & Spellman Architects
Designer: Crawford Dunn

3552 The City of Mesquite, Texas
Designer: Crawford Dunn

3553 Streams and Valleys Commission
Designer: Crawford Dunn

3554 Bank of Commerce
Designer: Crawford Dunn

3555 Texas Stadium
Designer: Crawford Dunn

3556 University of Texas at Arlington
Designer: Crawford Dunn

3557 Ft. Worth Chamber of Commerce
Designer: Crawford Dunn

3558 Deal Development Company
Designer: Crawford Dunn

3559 Dallas Museum of Fine Arts
& Ft. Worth Museum of Art
Designer: Crawford Dunn

3560 Datum Structures Engineers Inc.
Designer: Crawford Dunn

3561 Willow Creek Community Center
Designer: Al Burlini/Tom Morris, Inc.

3562 Lutheran General Hospital
Designer: Al Burlini/Tom Morris, Inc.

 3563

 3567

 3564

 3568

 3565

 3569

 3566

 3570

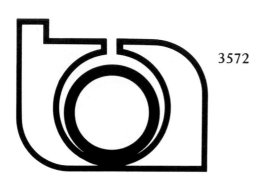

3571

3572

3573

3574

3563   Personalized Service Group
       Designer: Al Burlini; Tom Morris Inc.

3564   Young Life
       Designer: Al Burlini; Tom Morris, Inc.

3565   Des Plaines National Bank
       Designer: Al Burlini; Tom Morris, Inc.

3566   Sur International
       Designer: Triad Associates

3567   Cedar Ridge Estates
       Designer: Triad Associates

3568   Old Reliable Mortgage Co.
       Designer: Triad Associates

3569   Texas Food Merchant
       Designer: Triad Associates

3570   Bob Edwards Insurance & Real Estate
       Designer: Triad Associates

3571   Our Land, Our Lives . . . a Coalition
            for Human Rights
       Designer: Triad Associates

3572   Triad Associates
       Designer: Triad Associates

3573   The Windmill
       Designer: Triad Associates

3574   Hupp Systems, Inc.
       Designer: Triad Associates

 3575

 3579

 3576

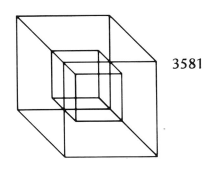 3580

 3577

 3581

 3578

 3582

3583

3584

ELK GROVE VILLAGE

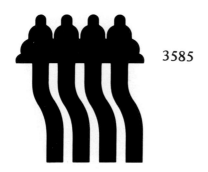

3585

3586

3575  Waco Printing and Stationery Company
      Designer: Triad Associates

3576  Riley's Midway Pharmacy, Inc.
      Designer: Triad Associates

3577  Garden Gate Apartments
      Designer: Triad Associates

3578  Mobile Home Service Co. of the Southwest
      Designer: Triad Associates

3579  TexasBank
      Designer: Triad Associates

3580  One Main Place, Texas Bank
      Designer: The Richards Group

3581  Robert H. Norris, Architect
      Designer: The Richards Group

3582  Exchange Bank
      Designer: The Richards Group

3583  Neuro Systems
      Designer: The Richards Group

3584  Elk Grove Village
      Designer: The Richards Group

3585  The Trails
      Designer: The Richards Group

3586  Varo, Inc.
      Designer: The Richards Group

 3587

 3591

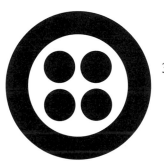 3588

 3592

 3589

 3593

 3590

 3594

3595

3596

3597

3598

3587  Cimarron Corporation
      Designer: The Richards Group

3588  The Men and Boys Clothing Association
      Designer: The Richards Group

3589  Hand Made Originals
      Designer: The Richards Group

3590  Chandlers Landing
      Designer: The Richards Group

3591  The Backroom Bar
      Designer: The Richards Group

3592  The Duffel and Ditty Restaurant
      Designer: The Richards Group

3593  Surveyor Companies
      Designer: The Richards Group

3594  Lakeside Village
      Designer: The Richards Group

3595  Chimney Hill
      Designer: The Richards Group

3596  Hillside Townhomes
      Designer: The Richards Group

3597  Pinewild Condominiums
      Designer: The Richards Group

3598  Channel 8 TV Station
      Designer: The Richards Group

3599

3603

3600

3604

3601

3605

3602

ESTRADA

3606

 3607

 3608

 3609

3610

3599 Stoneridge
Designer: The Richards Group

3600 Southern Methodist University
Designer: The Richards Group

3601 Earth Grains Bread
Designer: The Richards Group

3602 Estrada (the wine of Argentina)
Designer: The Richards Group

3603 Jack Unruh
Designer: The Richards Group

3604 USA Film Festival
Designer: The Richards Group

3605 Airborne Connectors
Designer: The Richards Group

3606 Dallas Alliance
Designer: The Richards Group

3607 Neiman Marcus
Designer: The Richards Group

3608 Channel 5 TV Station
Designer: The Richards Group

3609 Dallas Chamber of Commerce
Designer: The Richards Group

3610 Innisgate Townhomes
Designer: The Richards Group

**SUMMERTOP** 3611

A T   N O R T H P A R K

3612

*Dallastyle* 3613

3614
**THUNDER**

 3615

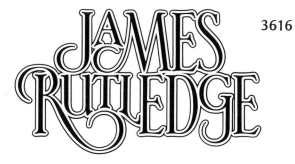 3616

3617

3618

3611  Northpark Shopping Center
      Designer: The Richards Group

3612  Nitzinger (rock group)
      Designer: The Richards Group

3613  Dallas Chamber of Commerce
      Designer: The Richards Group

3614  Thunder (rock group)
      Designer: The Richards Group

3615  Channel 13 — Educational TV Station
      Designer: The Richards Group

3616  James Rutledge (rock singer)
      Designer: The Richards Group

3617  Oz Restaurant
      Designer: The Richards Group

3618  Earth Grains Bread
      Designer: The Richards Group

PETER PIPER PLASTICS

3619

3623

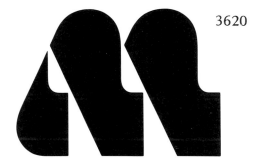

3620

3624

3621

3625

3622

3626

**3627**

**3628**

**3629**

**3630**

3619  Peter Piper Plastics
      Designer: The Richards Group

3620  Monesson and Company
      Designer: The Richards Group

3621  1972 USA Film Festival
      Designer: The Richards Group

3622  Bill Birdyshaw
      Designer: The Richards Group

3623  Canterbury Press
      Designer: The Richards Group

3624  The Crystal Forest Restaurant
      Designer: The Richards Group

3625  Earth Grains Bread
      Designer: The Richards Group

3626  Larry and Deawna Sons
      Designer: The Richards Group

3627  20th Century Fox
      Designer: The Richards Group

3628  East Park Shopping Mall
      Designer: The Richards Group

3629  One Up Restaurant
      Designer: The Richards Group

3630  La Cascada Restaurant
      Designer: The Richards Group

3631

3635

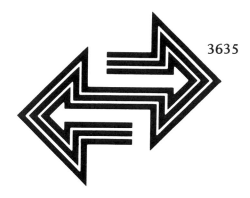

3632

3636

3633

3637

3634

STUD1O

3638

**3639**

**3640**

3631  Union Trust
Designer: The Richards Group

3632  Nevada Cement
Designer: The Richards Group

3633  Candle Ridge
Designer: The Richards Group

3634  Studio Ten Productions, Inc.
Designer: The Richards Group

3635  Equitable Relocation Service
Designer: Equitable Graphics

3636  GATX-Fuller Co.
Designer: Knapp Design Associates

3637  The Bendix Corporation
Designer: Lippincott & Margulies

3638  Twin Oaks Company
Designer: Bruce A. Cottingham

3639  Rhode Island Hospital Trust National Bank
Designer: Agnes Killabin

3640  Archer Daniels Midland Co.
Designer: Latham Tyler Jensen, Inc.

3641  Express International Travel Services
Designer: Mike Quon

3642  Management Research Institute
Designer: Mike Quon

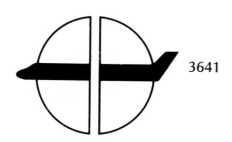

**3641**

**3642**

 3643

 3647

 3644

 3648

 3645

 3649

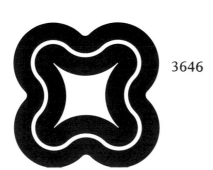 3646

 3650

 3651

 3652

 3653

 3654

3643  Sentry Medical Products
      Designer: Mike Quon

3644  International Geographic Society
      Designer: Mike Quon

3645  Vision Institute of America, Inc.
      Designer: Richard Howe; Overlock Howe & Co.

3646  Orbon Industries, Inc
      Designer: Richard Howe; Overlock Howe & Co.

3647  Goomba's Discotheque
      Designer: Richard Deardorff;
         Overlock Howe & Co.

3648  Tacony Distributors, Inc.
      Designer: Richard Deardorff;
         Overlock Howe & Co.

3649  Kalamazoo Center
      Designer: Richard Deardorff

3650  Bill's Tap & Restaurant
      Designer: Richard Deardorff

3651  St. Joseph High School Swim Club Boosters
      Designer: Richard Deardorff

3652  Area Resources Improvement Council
      Designer: Richard Deardorff

3653  Highland House Development
      Designer: Richard Deardorff

3654  Richard Petrie
      Designer: Richard Deardorff

 3655

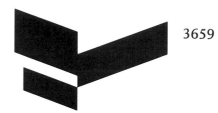 3659

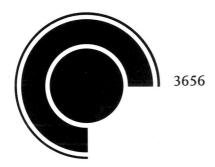 3656

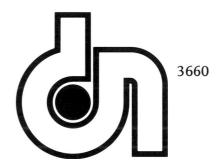 3660

 3657

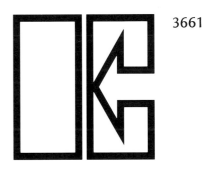 3661

GALLERY 615 3658

 3662

**3663**

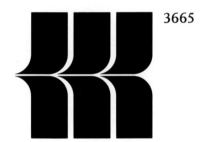

**3664**

**3665**

**3666**

3655  Tri County Community Action Program
Designer: Richard Deardorff

3656  Industrial Design Center, Whirlpool Corporation
Designer: Richard Deardorff

3657  Twin Cities Area Child Care Center
Designer: Richard Deardorff

3658  Gallery 615
Designer: Richard Deardorff

3659  Retail Marketing Department, Whirlpool Corp.
Designer: Richard Deardorff

3660  Donald Nupp Architectural Services
Designer: Richard Deardorff

3661  Information Center, Whirlpool Corporation
Designer: Richard Deardorff

3662  Lion & The Ram Beauty Salons
Designer: Richard Deardorff

3663  Blossomland United Way
Designer: Richard Deardorff

3664  The Samaritan Center
Designer: Richard Deardorff

3665  Economic & Marketing Research,
       Whirlpool Corporation
Designer: Richard Deardorff

3666  Planned Parenthood of Southwestern Michigan
Designer: Richard Deardorff

 3667

 3671

 3668

 3672

edd gerring/haircrafter

 3669

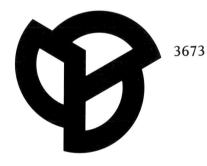 3673

3670

 3674

3675

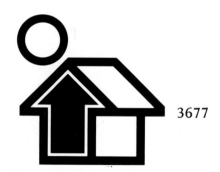

3676

3677

3678

3667  Technological Forecast, Whirlpool Corporation
      Designer: Richard Deardorff

3668  Project Seed, Whirlpool Corporation
      Designer: Richard Deardorff

3669  Grand Mere Association
      Designer: Richard Deardorff

3670  American Red Cross Youth
      Designer: Richard Deardorff

3671  Benton Harbor/Benton Harbor Township
         Model Cities Program
      Designer: Richard Deardorff

3672  Edd Gerring
      Designer: Richard Deardorff

3673  Southwestern Michigan Regional
         Planning Commission
      Designer: Richard Deardorff

3674  Patterson Printing
      Designer: Richard Deardorff

3675  The Man Alive
      Designer: Richard Deardorff

3676  Dwan Graphic Arts
      Designer: Richard Deardorff

3677  Town Homes, Inc.
      Designer: Richard Deardorff

3678  Wm. E. Mahaffay
      Designer: Richard Deardorff

 3679

 3683

 3680

UNCLES

 3684

 3681

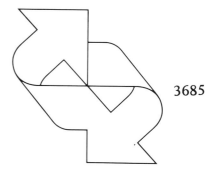 3685

 3682

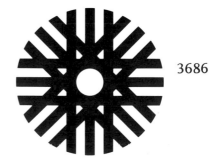 3686

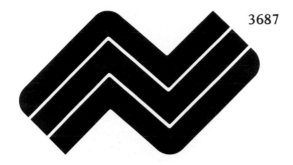

3687

3688

3689

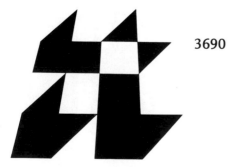

3690

3679 Oxidon 2000 (waste treatment system);
Whirlpool Corporation
Designer: Richard Deardorff

3680 St. Joseph, Michigan YMCA
Designer: Richard Deardorff

3681 Boultinghouse Photography
Designer: Richard Deardorff

3682 Cathedral School of the Arts
Designer: Richard Deardorff

3683 Kitchen Appliance Package Assembly;
Whirlpool Corporation
Designer: Richard Deardorff

3684 Nadele Alexia O'Donnel
Marketing Communications
Designer: Lans Bouthillier;
Corporate Design Systems

3685 Guidelines
Designer: Lans Bouthillier;
Corporate Design Systems

3686 Sun Savings & Loan Association
Designer: Richard Vieira
Corporate Design Systems

3687 National Plastifab
Designer: Lans Bouthillier;
Corporate Design Systems

3688 Cambridge Historical Commission
Designer: Richard Vieira;
Corporate Design Systems

3689 Rockingham Hotel
Designer: Ronald Couture;
Corporate Design Systems

3690 Saunders, Cheng & Appleton
Designer: Richard Vieira;
Corporate Design Systems

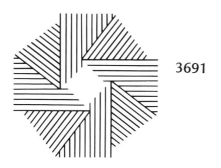 3691

 3695

 3692

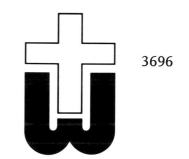 3696

 3693

 3697

 3694

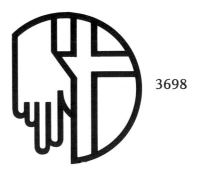 3698

 **3699**

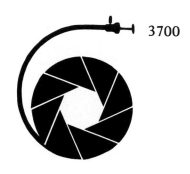 **3700**

 **3701**

 **3702**

3691  Interspace Inc.
Designer: Beverly Gilman;
Corporate Design Systems

3692  World Wildlife Fund
Designer: Lans Bouthillier;
Corporate Design Systems

3693  The Windrifter
Designer: Richard Vieira;
Corporate Design Systems

3694  Outer Banks Safari
Designer: Everett Forbes

3695  Mariner's Cove
Designer: Everett Forbes

3696  Warrington Presbyterian Church
Designer: Everett Forbes

3697  Schwartzschild Jewelers
Designer: Dudley Cook; Martin/Remick/Moore

3698  All Saints Episcopal Church
Designer: Dudley Cook; Martin/Remick/Moore

3699  New Life for Youth
Designer: Dudley Cook; Martin/Remick/Moore

3700  Greg Moore, Photographer
Designer: Dudley Cook; Martin/Remick/Moore

3701  First Mate Restaurants, Inc.
Designer: Jim Lake

3702  American Middle East Consultants
Designer: Jim Lake

3703

3707

3704

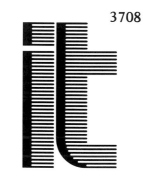

3708

3705

3709

3706

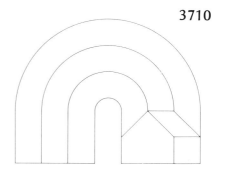

3710

**3711**

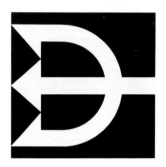

**3712**

**3713**

3703 Heimlich & Company
Designer: Jim Lake

3704 Perky Pet Products, Inc.
Designer: Jim Lake

3705 Magi-Tack, Inc.
Designer: Jim Lake

3706 Gemini International
Designer: Jim Lake

3707 Alco, Inc.
Designer: Jim Lake

3708 Institute of Trichology
Designer: The Company

3709 Modular Development Co.
Designer: The Company

3710 Brentwood Youth House
Designer: The Company

3711 George Meinzinger Photography
Designer: The Company

3712 Del Amo Marine
Designer: The Company

3713 Klein Englander contract furniture sales
Designer: The Company

**3714**

3714 Financial Marketing Corporation
Designer: The Company

3715

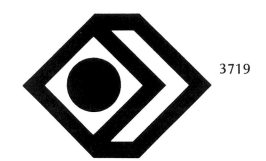

3719

3716

3720

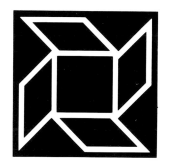

3717

3721

3718

3722

MountainGate

**3723**

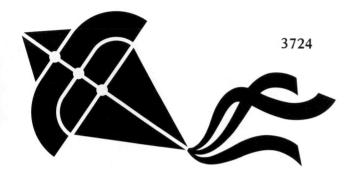

**3724**

**3725**

**3726**

3715 American Telecommunications Corp.
Designer: The Company

3716 Astrodata
Designer: The Company

3717 Allied Corregated Box Corp.
Designer: The Company

3718 Intercontinental Systems
Designer: The Company

3719 Video Security Systems
Designer: The Company

3720 Creative Capital Corporation
Designer: The Company

3721 Al's Garage (clothing)
Designer: Connie Beck;
    John Follis & Associates

3722 Mountaingate Country Club
Designer: Wayne Hunt/Elizabeth Baird;
    John Follis & Associates

3723 Village Palos Verdes
Designer: Wayne Hunt/Connie Beck;
    John Follis & Associates

3724 Village of Woodbridge
Designer: Elizabeth Baird;
    John Follis & Associates

3725 Carolina Copy Center
Designer: Bob Herr; Charles Crone & Assocs.

3726 October Galleries
Designer: Chip Clarke

3727

3731

3728

3732

3729

3733

THE **51** STATE  3730
CHANNEL **13**

3734

3735

3736

3737

3738

3727  Texasgulf Inc.
      Designer: George Tscherny

3728  R.L. Banks & Associates, Inc.
      Designer: George Tscherny

3729  Curtis Brown Ltd.
      Designer: George Tscherny

3730  Educational Broadcasting Co.
      Designer: George Tscherny

3731  Michael A. Schacht Inc.
      Designer: George Tscherny

3732  Setec — Weidlinger
      Designer: George Tscherny

3733  Design Built Exhibits, Inc.
      Designer: George Tscherny

3734  Community Vasectomy Clinic
      Designer: Ed Penniman

3735  The Wheel Works (pottery)
      Designer: Ed Penniman

3736  Todd Thal (Mercedes-Benz repair)
      Designer: Ed Penniman

3737  Victor Kemp Company
      Designer: Ed Penniman

3738  Center on Aging
      Designer: Calvin Woo

3739

3743

3740

3744

3741

3745

3742

3746

**3747**

**3748**

**3749**

3739  La Jolla Development Company
       Designer: Calvin Woo

3740  Woo Chee Chong, Inc. (oriental foods)
       Designer: Calvin Woo

3741  Grossmont Hospital
       Designer: Calvin Woo

3742  Shared Jobs
       Designer: Calvin Woo

3743  About Behavior Change Groups
       Designer: Calvin Woo

3744  Arizona Brake & Clutch, Inc.
       Designer: Calvin Woo

3745  Best Photo
       Designer: Calvin Woo

3746  W & M Plastics, Inc.
       Designer: Calvin Woo

3747  Starr Boltt, youth fashions
       Designer: Calvin Woo

3748  Dial Tube Company
       Designer: Patrick Benton

3749  Patrick Benton Advertising Design
       Designer: Patrick Benton

3750  The Art Club News
       Designer: Patrick Benton

**3750**

# The Art Club News

3751

3752

3753

3754

3755

3756

3757

3758

3759

3760

3761

3762

3751 American Commonwealth Financial Corp.
Designer: Patrick Benton

3752 KTLC Radio
Designer: Patrick Benton

3753 Splinter Pickle Co., Inc.
Designer: Victor DiCristo

3754 Cedarburg Recycling Program
Designer: Victor DiCristo

3755 Commercial Bank
Designer: Victor DiCristo

3756 DiCristo Design
Designer: Victor DiCristo

3757 Children's Service Soceity of Wisconsin
Designer: Victor DiCristo

3758 Madison Newspapers, Inc.
Designer: Victor DiCristo

3759 Freed's Stores
Designer: L.S. Krispinsky

3760 Executive Advertising
Designer: L.S. Krispinsky

3761 Academic Improvement Center
Designer: Don Primi

3762 Gabor J. Mertl & Assocs., Architects
Designer: Don Primi

 3763

 3767

 3764

  3768

 3765

3769

3766

 3770

3771

3772

3773

3774

3763  Hastings Pavement Co., Inc.
Designer: Don Primi

3764  Rocking K Cattle Corporation
Designer: Don Primi

3765  Nassau Crossways International Plaza
Designer: Don Primi

3766  Railmark, Ltd.
Designer: Don Primi

3767  The Hutter Agency
Designer: Don Primi

3768  PSI, Division of Phillis Sportswear, Inc.
Designer: Don Primi

3769  Community Bus Shelters, Inc.
Designer: Don Primi

3770  Barstow Medical Center
Designer: Don Primi

3771  Turo Construction Corp.
Designer: Don Primi

3772  Vironic Systems, Inc.
Designer: Don Primi

3773  Zale Properties, Inc.
Designer: Don Primi

3774  Temtech Designs Corp.
Designer: Don Primi

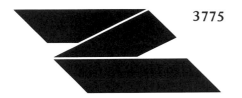
3775

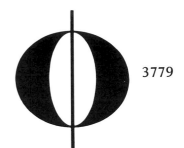
3779

3776

3780

3777

3781

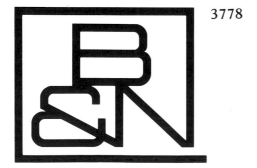
3778

3782

**3783**

**3784**

**3785**

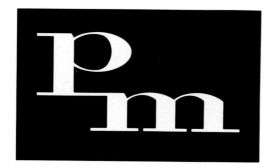

**3786**

3775  Zale Realty Corp.
Designer: Don Primi

3776  Carol Bachman, Interior Design
Designer: Don Primi

3777  Louis Vynerib & Associates, Inc.
Designer: Don Primi

3778  Blum & Nerzig, Architects
Designer: Don Primi

3779  Phi Equities Corp.
Designer: Don Primi

3780  Quakertown Brick & Tile Co., Inc.
Designer: Don Primi

3781  Victory Corporation
Designer: Don Primi

3782  Credit Card Exchange
Designer: Don Primi

3783  Arthur J. Taft Co.
Designer: Don Primi

3784  Compac, Inc.
Designer: Don Primi

3785  Perry Meyers, Inc.
Designer: Don Primi

3786  Property Management Associates, Inc.
Designer: Don Primi

3787

3788

3789

3790

3791

# Cherokee
# Brick

3792

3787  Trans-Ad, Ltd.
      Designer: Don Primi

3788  Target Rock Corporation
      Designer: Don Primi

3789  Penn-State Corporation
      Designer: Don Primi

3790  Leisure Distributors, Inc.
      Designer: Don Primi

3791  Cherokee Brick Co. of North Carolina
      Designer: Don Primi

3792  Tele-Communications Consultants, Inc.
      Designer: Don Primi

3793  Arley Properties Co.
      Designer: Don Primi

3794  Syscon Corporation
      Designer: Don Primi

3793

# ARLEY
# PROPERTIES
# COMPANY

3794

3795

**LAS** 3796

3799

**rhs** 3797

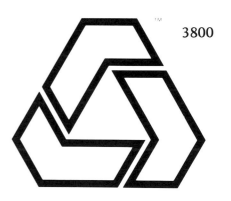
3800

3798

**INTERLOC**

 3801

 3802

 3803

3804

3795 Evans Clay Products, Inc.
Designer: Don Primi

3796 Lee A. Sagistano, AIA Architect
Designer: Don Primi

3797 Michael Harris Spector & Assocs., Architects
Designer: Don Primi

3798 Interloc Realty Co.
Designer: Don Primi

3799 Bamberger Polymers, Inc.
Designer: Don Primi

3800 Triangle Brick Co.
Designer: Don Primi

3801 David Manufacturing Co.
Designer: David M. Murphy

3802 Southeast Ohio Emergency Medical Services
Designer: Dean R. Lindsay

3803 Dairy Council of Georgia, Inc.
Designer: Judy Gazaway; Atvur Associates

3804 Pinewood Plantation
Designer: Savas Atvur; Atvur Associates

3805

3809

3806

3810

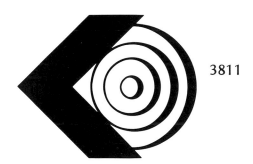

3807

3811

3808

3812

# STOTTER <sup>3813</sup>

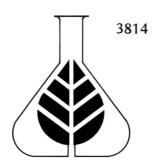

**3814**

**FISCHER**X·RAY **3815**

**3816**

3805 Lanier Island Cottages
Designer: J.C. James; Atvur Associates

3806 Kuruna
Designer: Judy Gazaway; Atvur Associates

3807 Davenport
Designer: Savas Atvur; Atvur Associates

3808 Southern Nature, Div. of Mar Beau, Inc.
Designer: Orien O. Hall, II; Atvur Associates

3809 Troy Davis & Associates
Designer: Richard Beauchamp; Atvur Assocs.

3810 Wright of Thomasville
Thomasville, North Carolina

3811 Food Marketing Inc.
Designer: Design Consultants, Inc.

3812 Stylex '74 Exhibitors, Inc.
Designer: Design Consultants, Inc.

3813 H.J. Stotter Inc.
Designer: Cheryl Adams Darson;
Design Consultants, Inc.

3814 Agrand, Ltd.
Designer: Design Consultants, Inc.

3815 H.G. Fischer Inc.
Designer: Design Consultants, Inc.

3816 Cudahy Foods Co.
Designer: Design Consultants, Inc.

the cheese shop 3817

the meat market 3821

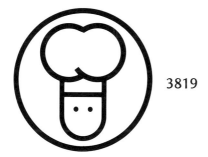

the international café 3818

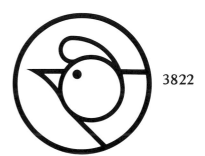

the poultry market 3822

the cooking counter 3819

the produce market 3823

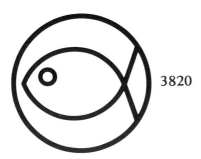

the fish market 3820

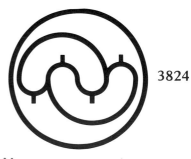

the sausage shop 3824

3825

3826

3827

3817—3824  Series of symbols for
              Market Place
              Designer: Anthony Aviles;
              Harper + George

3825  Treetops Condominiums
      Designer: Anthony Aviles;
      Harper + George

3826  Jonynas and Shephard, Stained
      Glass Window Designers
      Designer: Anthony Aviles;
      Harper + George

3827  Marvil Gelman, Lighting Consultant
      Designer: Anthony Aviles;
      Harper + George

3828  New York State Democtatic 1974
      Fund Raising Committee
      Designer: Anthony Aviles;
      Harper + George

3828

Coffee Garden 3829

3833

3830

Pool Deck

3834

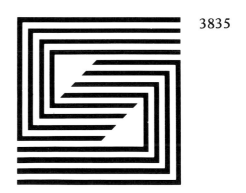

3831

Health Club

3835

New York City
Diamond Jubilee
1898-1973

3832

Bronx Brooklyn Manhattan Queens Richmond

3836

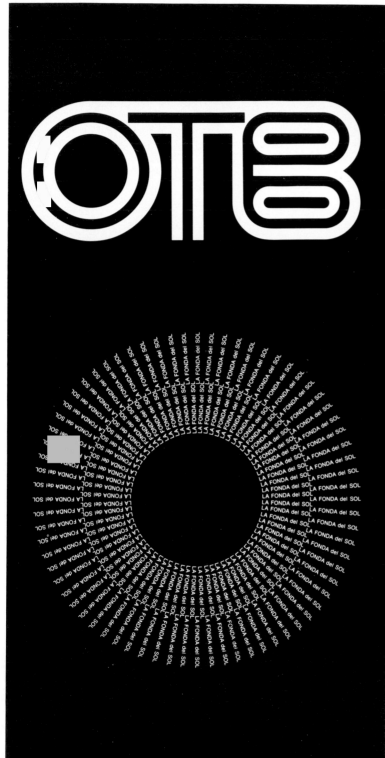

 3839

 3843

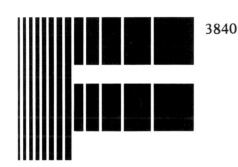 3840

 3844

 3841

 3845

 3841

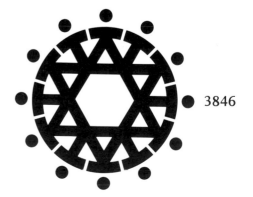 3846

# EverFlex  3847

3848

3849

3839 United Jewish Federation 75th Anniversary
Designer: Stan Brod

3840 Filmakers to Go
Designer: Stan Brod

3841 Wise Temple
Designer: Stan Brod

3842 Gordon M. Bogdan Real Estate Developers
Designer: Stan Brod

3843 Evercoat
Designer: Stan Brod

3844 Natl. Assn. for Creative Children & Adults
Designer: Stan Brod

3845 Voters for Gilligan
Designer: Stan Brod

3846 Hillel Academy
Designer: Stan Brod

3847 EverFlex
Designer: Stan Brod

3848 Lighthouse Runaway Shelter
Designer: Stan Brod

3849 Wyoming May Fete
Designer: Stan Brod

3850 B'nai Avraham Northern Hills Synagogue
Designer: Stan Brod

3850

 3851

 3855

 3852

 3856

 3853

 3857

 3854

 3858

Western Pacific
Financial Corporation

**3859**

**3860**

**3861**

**3862**

3851   Interim, Inc.
        Designer: Gale William Ikola

3852   Don G. Lee and Associates
        Designer: Gale William Ikola

3853   Special Blue Dot Springs
        Designer: Gale William Ikola

3854   Minnesota Zoological Society
        Designer: Gale William Ikola

3855   F & M Savings Bank
        Designer: Gale William Ikola

3856   Shippers Supply Co.
        Designer: Jack E. Kannapell, Jr.

3857   Mockingbird Valley Racquet Club
        Designer: Jack E. Kannapell, Jr.

3858   Western Pacific Financial Corporation
        Designer: Mike Kaiser

3859   Decision 75 — Sherman Oaks Lutheran Church
        Designer: Daniel M. Partain

3860   Redd Foxx Productions
        Designer: Daniel M. Partain

3861   Audio Tek (recording studio)
        Designer: Cyril John Schlosser

3862   Jim Burns (airbrush specialist)
        Designer: Cyril John Schlosser

3863

3867

3864

3868

3865

3869

3866

PHOENIX
CIVIC PLAZA

3670

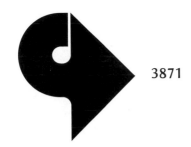

3871

3872

3873

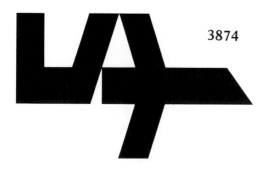

3874

3863  Northeast Residence, Inc.
Designer: Cyril John Schlosser

3864  Dietrich Company
Designer: Cyril John Schlosser

3865  Sierra School of the Bible
Designer: Don Sterrenburg

3866  Immanuel Baptist Church
Designer: Don Sterrenburg

3867  Compugraphic Corporation, Type Div.
Designer: Don Sterrenburg

3868  Cedar Creek Festival of Arts & Crafts
Designer: Victor DiCristo

3869  Jack Burktenica/Landscape Architect
Designer: Ernest H. Stedman;
    E.H. Stedman Graphic Design

3870  Phoenix Civic Plaza
Designer: Ernest H. Stedman;
    E.H. Stedman Graphic Design

3871  Cooper Architectural Signs
Designer: Ernest H. Stedman;
    E.H. Stedman Graphic Design

3872  Howard F. Thompson, Architect
Designer: Ernest H. Stedman;
    E.H. Stedman Graphic Design

3873  Pacific Design Center
Designer: Ernest H. Stedman;
    Rex Goode Organization for Design

3874  Los Angeles International Airport
Designer: Ernest H. Stedman;
    E.H. Stedman Graphic Design

 3875

 3879

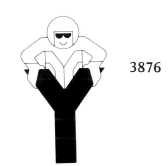 3876

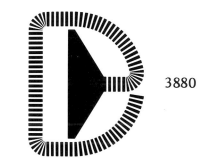 3880

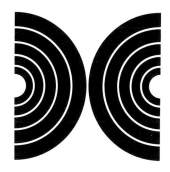 3877

 3881

 3878

 3882

**3883**

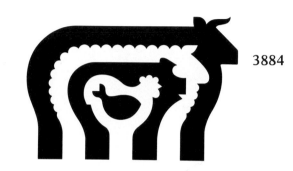

**3884**

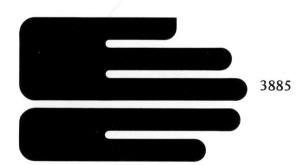

**3885**

**3886**

3875 Sequoia Pacific
Designer: Ken Chapman;
Rex Goode Organization for Design

3876 Yamaha Learn to Ride Program
Designer: Carlos Huerta/Roger Johnson;
Huerta Design

3877 Design Communications
Designer: Roger Johnson; Huerta Design

3878 Asanuma
Designer: Roger Johnson; Huerta Design

3879 The Art Group
Designer: Roger Johnson; Huerta Design

3880 Doyle Group
Designer: Roger Johnson; Huerta Design

3881 National Credit Information Services
Designer: Jim Potocki; Huerta Design

3882 Cornell Bridgers & Troller
Designer: Roger Johnson; Huerta Design

3883 International Cycle House
Designer: Carlos Huerta/Roger Johnson;
Huerta Design

3884 Arroyo Foods
Designer: Roger Johnson; Huerta Design

3885 Extended Care Facilities, Inc.
Designer: Roger Johnson; Huerta Design

3886 Knott's Berry Farm
Designer: Carlos Huerta/Roger Johnson;
Huerta Design

 3887

SIDE STREET

 3888

 3889

 3890

**3891**

**3892**

**3893**

3887  Giannelli
      Designer: Carlos Huerta; Huerta Design

3888  Art Directors Club of Los Angeles
      Designer: Roger Johnson; Huerta Design

3889  Watson Industrial Center
      Designer: Octavio Huerta/Roger Johnson;
         Huerta Design

3890  Tyco Industries
      Designer: Hector Huerta/Roger Johnson;
         Huerta Design

3891  Statakil Corporation
      Designer: Roger Johnson; Huerta Design

3892  Pioneer French Baking Co.
      Designer: Roger Johnson; Huerta Design

3893  Huerta Design Associates
      Designer: Hector Huerta/Roger Johnson;
         Huerta Design

3894  Liquidity Fund, Inc.
      Designer: Jim Potocki; Huerta Design

**3894**

 3895

 3899

 3896

 3900

 3897

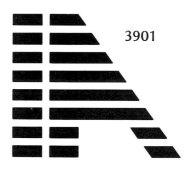 3901

 3898

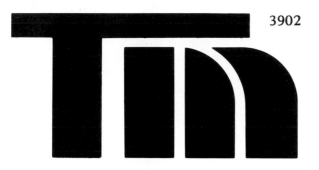

3902

3903

3904

3895 Bob Crane & Assocs., Realtor
Designer: Jim Potocki; Jim Potocki & Assocs.

3896 Ross Loos Medical Group
Designer: Carlos Huerta/Roger Johnson;
Huerta Design

3897 E. Clark Starr, Graphic Design
Designer: E. Clark Starr

3898 The Galleon & Gallery Ltd.
Designer: E. Clark Starr

3899 American Sawing and Drilling Co., Inc.
Designer: E. Clark Starr

3900 New England Alumni Trust
Designer: E. Clark Starr

3901 Input Applications Inc.
Designer: E. Clark Starr

3902 Team Marketing Corporation
Designer: E. Clark Starr

3903 The Killdear Society
Designer: Elaine M. Lyerly;
Monte J. Curry Marketing

3904 Exhibit World, Inc.
Designer: Monte J. Curry

3905 Nathaniel Hill and Associates
Designer: Monte J. Curry

3905

 3906

 3910

DIAL•A•RECIPE

 3907

Layne

 3911

the BeaHive

 3908

 3912

 3909

englewood
Pride in its People

3913

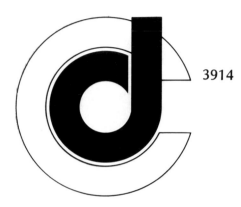

3914

3906 News Release Service
Designer: Elaine M. Lyerly

3907 Layne-Trane Service
Designer: Monte J. Curry

3908 Caralou Callissi Cirillo, Interior Designer
Designer: Kay Ritta

3909 Englewood (city symbol)
Designer: Kay Ritta

3910 Dial-A-Recipe
Designer: Kay Ritta

3915

3911 The BeaHive
Designer: Kay Ritta

3912 Englewood Independent Alliance
Designer: Kay Ritta

The Family Bank

3913 Huk-A-Poo
Designer: Kay Ritta

3914 Circle D
Designer: Paul Turzio

3916

3915 The Family Bank
Designer: John H. Harland Co.

3916 Granite City Bank
Designer: John H. Harland Co.

**Family Financial
Center**

3917

3921

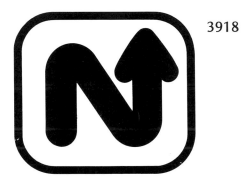

3918

3922

3919

3923

3920

3924

3925

3926

3917  Bank of Clarksdale
      Designer: John H. Harland Co.

3918  North St. Louis Trust Co.
      Designer: John H. Harland Co.

3919  Vic Womack & Associates, Inc.
      Designer: Point Communications, Inc.

3920  Laver-Emerson Fun'Set Vacations
      Designer: Point Communications, Inc.

3921  Rod Laver's LET/SET Resorts, Inc.
      Designer: Point Communications, Inc.

3922  American Assn. of Real Estate Boards, Inc.
      Designer: David Rainey

3923  The College of Cosmetology
      Designer: David Rainey

3924  The Great American Pant Co.
      Designer: David Rainey

3925  Steve Altman Photography
      Designer: David Rainey

3926  Mentor, Inc., Financial Consultants
      Designer: David Rainey

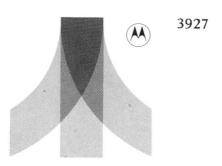
3927

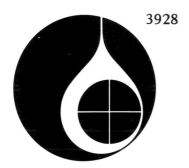
3928

3929

3930

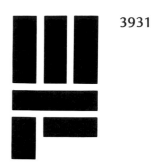
3931

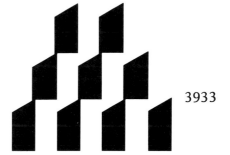
3932

3933

3934

 **3935**

 **3936**

 **3937**

 **3938**

3927 Motorola, Inc./Quasar
Designer: Visual Design Center, Inc.

3928 General Biologicals Co.
Designer: Visual Design Center, Inc.

3929 United Airlines Jetarama Theater
Designer: Visual Design Center, Inc.

3930 J.A. Olson Co.
Designer: Visual Design Center, Inc.

3931 Walter Frank Organization
Designer: Visual Design Center, Inc.

3932 Baldwin & Howell Companies
Designer: Michael Vanderbyl

3933 Hogland & Bogart
Designer: Michael Vanderbyl

3934 KTVU, Channel 2
Designer: Michael Vanderbyl/Dean Smith

3935 Transamerica Corp. (for employee magazine)
Designer: Michael Vanderbyl

3936 Mitchell Sails
Designer: Michael Vanderbyl

3937 AMCOM
Designer: Michael Vanderbyl

3938 Environmental Measurements
Designer: Michael Vanderbyl

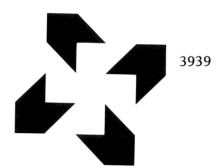

3939

3943

3940

3944

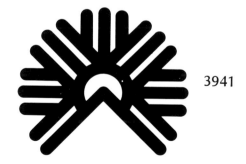

3941

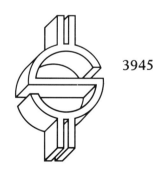

3945

3942

3946

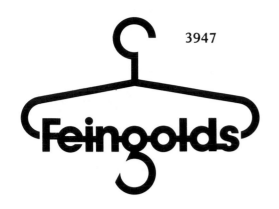

**3947**

**3948**

**3949**

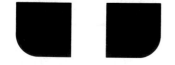

**3950**

3939 Hospital Consortium, Inc.
Designer: Michael Vanderbyl

3940 The Tischer Company
Designer: Michael Vanderbyl

3941 Alpine Villa Development Co.
Designer: Michael Vanderbyl

3942 The Yachtsmans Exchange
Designer: Michael Vanderbyl

3943 Five Star Insurance Plan
Designer: Jim Maccaroni; Parker Allen Co., Inc.

3944 Advertising Typographers
Designer: Jim Maccaroni; Parker Allen Co., Inc.

3945 Economic Counselors, Inc.
Designer: Philip Sehenuk; Parker Allen Co., Inc.

3946 Kragwood Broadcasting Inc.
Designer: Doug Powell; Image Group

3947 Feingolds Mens Wear
Designer: Doug Powell; Image Group

3948 Recreational Environments Consultants
Designer: Doug Powell; Image Group

3949 Jerry's of Chico
Designer: Charles Osborn; Image Group

3950 Health Manpower Council, Northeastern Calif.
Designer: Charles Osborn/Donald Price;
    Image Group

 3951

 3955

 3952

 3956

 3953

 3957

 3954

 3958

SACRAMENTO
HEARING SOCIETY INC.

**3959**

**3960**

**3961**

**3962**

3951 Organic Nutrients Inc.
Designer: John Gregg Berryman; Image Group

3952 The Metamorphis
Designer: John Gregg Berryman; Image Group

3953 Butte Creek Vineyards
Designer: John Gregg Berryman; Image Group

3954 Craig Hall Complex
Designer: John Gregg Berryman; Image Group

3955 Nortel Federal Credit Union
Designer: John Gregg Berryman; Image Group

3956 The Maltese Falcon
Designer: John Gregg Berryman; Image Group

3957 Organic Nutrients Inc.
Designer: John Gregg Berryman; Image Group

3958 Sacraments Hearing Society
Designer: Gaylord Bennitt/Steve Madeira

3959 Xandor Recording Studios
Designer: Charles R. Thomas

3960 Design Depot
Designer: Doug Powell; Image Group

3961 Sundance Records
Designer: David Bacigalupi

3962 Fort Sutter Hearing Aids
Designer: Gaylord Bennitt/Valerie Woo

 3963

 3967

 3964

3968

3965

3969

3966

COMMUNITY/CONVENTION CENTER

3970

**3971**

**3972**

**3973**

**3974**

3963 Calif. Div. of Tourism Development
   Designer: Gaylord Bennitt/
      Ted Thames

3964 Buffalo Brewing Co.
   Designer: John Gregg Berryman/
      Gaylord Bennitt

3965 Norwood Village
   Designer: Doug Powell; Image Group

3966 Sacramento Convention Center
   Designer: Gaylord Bennitt/Steve Madeira

3967 Sportsden
   Designer: G. Bennitt/J.G. Berryman

3968 Sacramento Amer. Rev. Bicentennial
   Designer: Gaylord Bennitt

3969 Johnston & Murphy Shoe Co.
   Designer: Brad Whitfield; Design Graphics

3970 Hospital Corp. of America, Intl. Division
   Designer: Hermann F. Zimmermann
      Design Graphics

3971 Nashville Musical Instruments Co.
   Designer: Bill Dick; Design Graphics

3972 Cromwell and Co.
   Designer: Bill Dick; Design Graphics

3973 Horace Small Co.
   Designer: Hermann F. Zimmermann;
      Design Graphics

3974 Johnston & Murphy Shoe Co.
   Designer: Brad Whitfield; Design Graphics

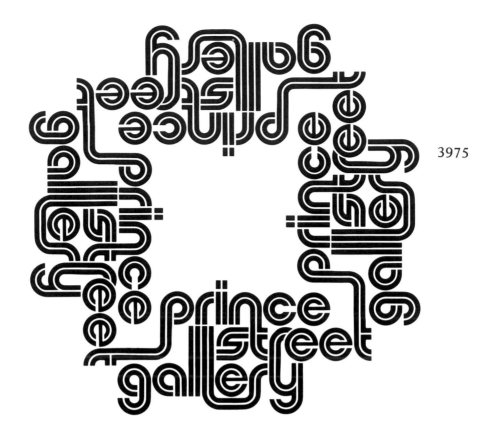

3975

3976

3977

3978

3979

3980

3981

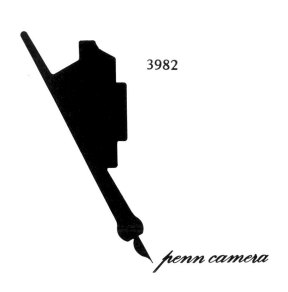

3982

*penn camera*

3985

3986

court clothes

3983

3987

USFunding Corporation

3984

**Citizens for Highway Safety**

3988

The COUNTRY COBBLER

3989

3990

3991

3992

3982 Penn Camera
Designer: John G. Cutler

3983 Travel-Van Camper
Designer: John G. Cutler

3984 Citizens for Highway Safety
Designer: Gray Whyte Design House, Inc.

3985 North Jersey Blood Center
Designer: Gray Whyte Design House, Inc.

3986 Court Clothes, Ltd.
Designer: Gray Whyte Design House, Inc.

3987 US Funding Corporation
Designer: Gray Whyte Design House, Inc.

3988 The Country Cobbler
Designer: Gray Whyte Design House, Inc.

3989 Gray Whyte Design House, Inc.
Designer: Gray Whyte Design House, Inc.

3990 Tyo Publishers
Designer: Pat Taylor, Inc.

3991 Carley Capital Group, Inc.
Designer: Pat Taylor, Inc.

3992 Airy View Condominium
Designer: Pat Taylor, Inc.

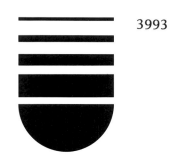

3993

3997

3994

3998

3995

3999

3996

OPTICOMP

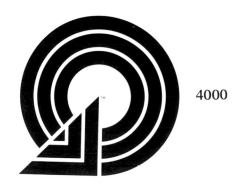

4000

4001

4002

4003

4004

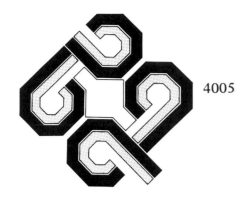
4005

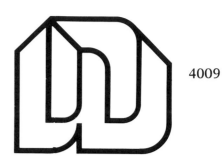
4009

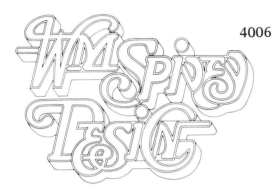
4006

4010

Banco de Venezuela

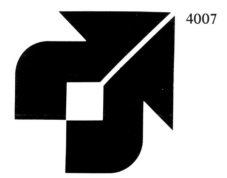
4007

4011

4008

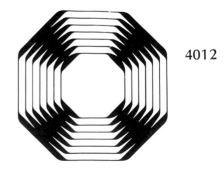
4012

4013

4014

4015

4016

4005 John Bates Architects
Designer: Wm Spivey Design

4006 Wm Spivey Design
Designer: Wm Spivey Design

4007 Promotora Venezolano Alemana
Designer: Jesus Emilio Franco

4008 Mini Drug
Designer: Jesus Emilio Franco

4009 Nancy Wilson - personal
Designer: Jesus Emilio Franco

4010 Banco de Venezuela
Designer: Jesus Emilio Franco

4011 Banco de Comercio
Designer: Jesus Emilio Franco

4012 C.A. La Electricidad de Caracas
Designer: Jesus Emilio Franco

4013 Villas del Mar
Designer: Jesus Emilio Franco

4014 Crenca
Designer: Jesus Emilio Franco

4015 Arquitectura Beckhoff
Designer: Jesus Emilio Franco

4016 Banco Provincial
Designer: Jesus Emilio Franco

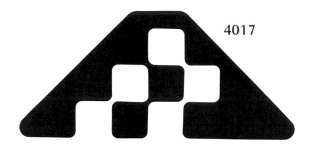 4017

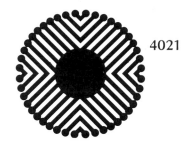 4021

 4018

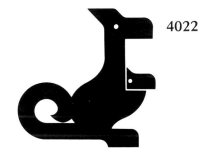 4022

**TENSIDOR** 4019

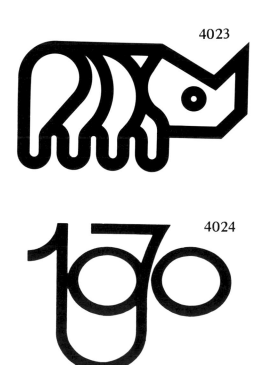 4023

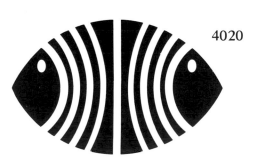 4020

4024

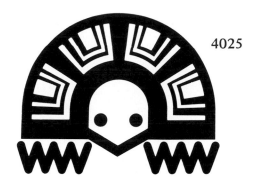

**4025**

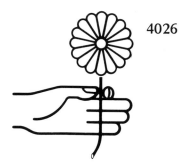

**4026**

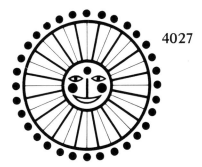

**4027**

**4028**

4017 La Piramide
Designer: Jesus Emilio Franco

4018 Caracas 400 Anos
Designer: Jesus Emilio Franco

4019 Tensidor
Designer: Jesus Emilio Franco

4020 Camuri Mar
Designer: Jesus Emilio Franco

4021 Primer Congreso de Medicina Interna
Designer: Jesus Emilio Franco

4022 Vivica
Designer: Jesus Emilio Franco

4023 Vigilancia y Transportes de Seguridad
Designer: Jesus Emilio Franco

4024 Calendario Grey's
DEsigner: Jesus Emilio Franco

4025 Prado Guayana
Designer: Jesus Emilio Franco

4026 Humanizacion de Caracas
Designer: Jesus Emilio Franco

4027 Leche los Teques
Designer: Jesus Emilio Franco

4028 Onda Nueva
Designer: Jesus Emilio Franco

 4029

 4033

 4030

 4034

 4031

 4035

 4032

4036

4037

4038

4039

4040

CARIBBEAN
HOTEL

4029  Produzco
      Designer: Jesus Emilio Franco

4030  Prado Humboldt
      Designer: Jesus Emilio Franco

4031  Banc Obrero
      Designer: Jesus Emilio Franco

4032  Tobacos La Cumanesa
      Designer: Jesus Emilio Franco

4033  Empaques Clement
      Designer: Jesus Emilio Franco

4034  Parques & Recreacion
      Designer: Jesus Emilio Franco

4035  Hideca
      Designer: Jesus Emilio Franco

4036  Centro Simon Bolivar
      Designer: Jesus Emilio Franco

4037  Arca-Centro Comercial
      Designer: Jesus Emilio Franco

4038  Los Desarollistas
      Designer: Jesus Emilio Franco

4039  San Felipe
      Designer: Jesus Emilio Franco

4040  Caribbean Hotel
      Designer: Jesus Emilio Franco

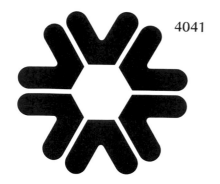

4041

4045

4042

4046

4043

4047

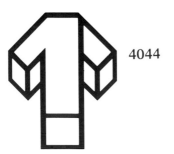

4044

4048

**4049**

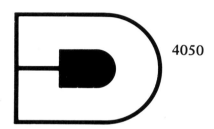

**4050**

**4051**

**4052**

4041 Minesterio de Obras Publicas
Designer: Jesus Emilio Franco

4042 Pata Pata — Zapateria
Designer: Jesus Emilio Franco

4043 Novgorod — Restaurant
Designer: Jesus Emilio Franco

4044 Tecnica Uno
Designer: Jesus Emilio Franco

4045 Productora de Grasas — El Dorado
Designer: Jesus Emilio Franco

4046 Solcasa
Designer: Jesus Emilio Franco

4047 Technical Financing
Designer: Jesus Emilio Franco

4048 Banco Nacional de Descuento
Designer: Jesus Emilio Franco

4049 Avicine
Designer: Jesus Emilio Franco

4050 Ernesto D'escrivan
Designer: Jesus Emilio Franco

4051 Automercados Global
Designer: Jesus Emilio Franco

4052 Banco Hipotecario del Este
Designer: Jesus Emilio Franco

 4053

 4057

 4054

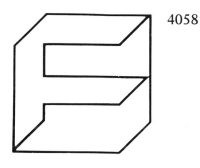 4058

 4055

 4059

 4056

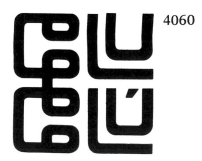 4060

**4061**

**4062**

**4063**

**4064**

4053  Capra
      Designer: Jesus Emilio Franco

4054  Clement
      Designer: Jesus Emilio Franco

4055  Centro Villasmal
      Designer: Jesus Emilio Franco

4056  Viveros Urimare
      Designer: Jesus Emilio Franco

4057  Optica Caracas
      Designer: Jesus Emilio Franco

4058  Forum
      Designer: Jesus Emilio Franco

4059  Rendimax
      Designer: Jesus Emilio Franco

4060  Glu Glu
      Designer: Jesus Emilio Franco

4061  La Floresta — Instuto Medico
      Designer: Jesus Emilio Franco

4062  Golden House
      Designer: Jesus Emilio Franco

4063  Centro Comercial Chacaito
      Designer: Jesus Emilio Franco

4064  Air Parts
      Designer: Jesus Emilio Franco

4065

4069

essex

4066

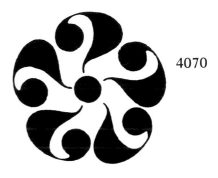
4070

4067

4071

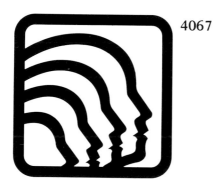

4068

happiness
launderers + dry cleaners
4072

 4073

 4074

Waugh Controls 4075

4076

4065 Andres Rosa - Personal
Designer: Jesus Emilio Franco

4066 Northeast Regional Center for
Rural Development — Cornell Univ.
Designer: James Estes

4067 Dept. of Human Development & Family
Studies — Cornell University
Designer: James Estes

4068 Graphic Productions
Designer: Cutro Associates

4069 Essex Lighting Co.
Designer: Cutro Associates

4070 How Graphics, Inc.
Designer: Cutro Associates

4071 Amber Aluminium Co.
Designer: Cutro Associates

4072 Happiness Launders & Dry Cleaners
Designer: Tim Oei Ing King

4073 Oei Ing King Design
Designer: Tim Oei Ing King

4074 Seven Enterprises Ltd.
Designer: Tim Oei Ing King

4075 Waugh Controls
Designer: Charles C. Waugh

4076 Blalack, Loop & Townsend
Designer: Stan Hutchinson;
Selje, Bond & Stewart

 4077

 4081

 4078

 4082

 4079

The
BEN JONSON

 4083

4084

The Chronicle
GRANITE AT LAKE · PASADENA
4080

4085

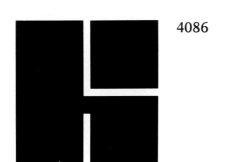

4086

4087

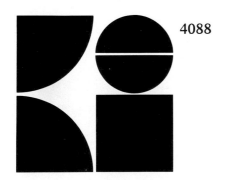

4088

4077 Intrapak Pacific
    Designer: Stan Hutchinson;
        Selje, Bond & Stewart

4078 Ten Downing Restaurant
    Designer: Stan Hutchinson;
        Selje, Bond & Stewart

4079 The Ben Jonson Restaurant (Lawry's)
    Designer: Stu Denker; Selje, Bond & Stewart

4080 The Chronicle Restaurant
    Designer: Gary Moore; Selje, Bond & Stewart

4081 Architectural Woodworking Co.
    Designer: Stan Hutchinson/Skip Morrow;
        Selje, Bond & Stewart

4082 Applewhite Mortgage Co.
    Designer: Skip Morrow;
        Selje, Bond & Stewart

4083 Nichols Family
    Designer: Larry Nichols;
        Emerson/Franzke Advertising, Inc.

4084 Kansas Power & Light Co., 50th Anniversary
    Designer: Larry Nichols;
        Emerson/Franzke Advertising, Inc.

4085 The Jockey Club
    Designer: Larry Nichols;
        Emerson/Franzke Advertising, Inc.

4086 Hester Industries, Inc.
    Designer: Randall R. Roth

4087 Stuermer, Architect
    Designer: Randall R. Roth

4088 Kiwanis International
    Designer: Randall R. Roth

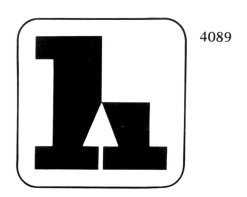 4089

 4093

**American Trauma Society**

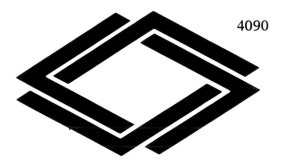 4090

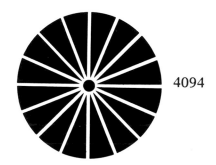 4094

 4091

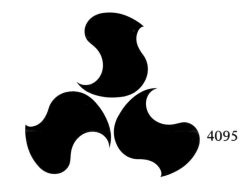 4095

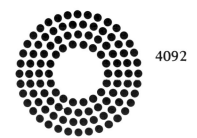 4092

 4096

**CHARLESTON, SOUTH CAROLINA**

4097

4098

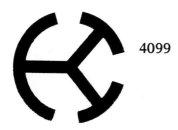

4099

4100

4089  Hardacre Real Estate
      Designer: Randall R. Roth

4090  Diamond Rubber Products, Inc.
      Designer: Don Davis Design

4091  Don Davis Design
      Designer: Don Davis Design

4092  Quincy's 23rd Annual Art Show
      Designer: Don Davis Design

4093  American Trauma Society
      Designer: Dennis Ichiyama

4094  Tokyo International Airport
      Designer: Dennis Ichiyama

4095  Radio WYEP
      Designer: Dennis Ichiyama

4096  Tenco Enterprises
      Designer: Dennis Ichiyama

4097  Charleston County Public Schools
      Charleston, South Carolina

4098  First National Bank of Clearwater
      Designer: Ensslin Advertising Agency

4099  Equity Oil Co.
      Designer: J. P. Denner & Assocs.

4100  Hudson Home Publications
      Designer: Otto Werk

4101

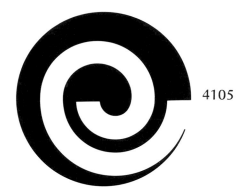

4105

4102

4106

4103

4107

4104

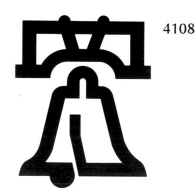

4108

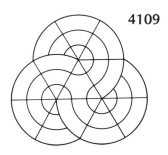

**4109**

**4110**

**4111**

**4112**

4101  Glen Ridge Congregational Church
Designer: Bill Wood; Design Shop

4102  Friends on the Phone
Designer: Bill Wood; Design Shop

4103  Shalebrook Realty
Designer: Bill Wood; Design Shop

4104  Dymecki Construction Co.
Designer: Bill Wood; Design Shop

4105  Scientific Incineration Devices, Inc.
Designer: Bill Wood; Design Shop

4106  Center for Parish Development
Designer: Bill Wood; Design Shop

4107  Everest Realty
Designer: Bill Wood; Design Shop

4108  Equal Opportunity Employment Service
Designer: Bill Wood; Design Shop

4109  Rogers College
Designer: Bill Wood; Design Shop

4110  Rogers College
Designer: Bill Wood; Design Shop

4111  Cherenson, Carroll & Holzer, Public Relations
Designer: Bill Wood; Design Shop

4112  Channel Companies, Inc.
Designer: Bill Wood; Design Shop

 4113

 4117

 4114

 4118

 4115

 4119

 4116

 4120

**4121**

**4122**

**4123**

**4124**

4113 Kings Fairground Mall
Designer: Bill Wood; Design Shop

4114 MidAtlantic Mortgage Co.
Designer: Bill Wood; Design Shop

4115 The Design Shop
Designer: Bill Wood; Design Shop

4116 Glen Ridge Bicentennial Committee
Designer: Bill Wood; Design Shop

4117 Investors General Estate Corp.
Designer: Bill Wood; Design Shop

4118 Community Corporation of America
Designer: Bill Wood; Design Shop

4119 Building and Land Technology Corp.
Designer: Bill Wood; Design Shop

4120 Acu-Tech Corp.
Designer: Bill Wood; Design Shop

4121 Educational Data Sciences, Inc.
Designer: Bill Wood; Design Shop

4122 Brown-Fowler Company Realtors
Designer: Bill Wood; Design Shop

4123 Green Gallery
Designer: Bill Wood; Design Shop

4124 L & L Mechanical Contractors, Inc.
Designer: Roland L. Lee; Ink Well

 4125

 4129

 4126

4130

 4127

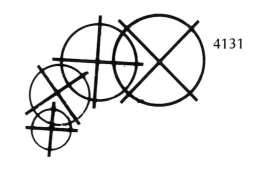 4131

 4128

 4132

**4133**

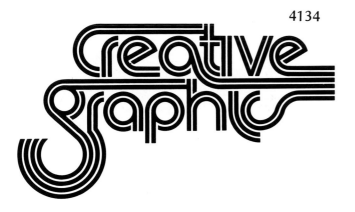

**4134**

4125 Wes Burke Realty
Designer: Roland L. Lee; Ink Well

4126 Sunrise Village Townhomes
Designer: Roland L. Lee; Ink Well

4127 Dixie Ambassadors
Designer: Roland L. Lee; Ink Well

4128 The Rafters Restaurant
Designer: Roland L. Lee; Ink Well

4129 Western Food Sales, Inc.
Designer: Roland L. Lee; Ink Well

4130 Highlands High School, Class of '76
Designer: Michael Draper

4131 Draper Enterprise Inc.
Designer: R.A. Draper, Sr.

4132 Robert A. Draper Advertising
Designer: R.A. Draper Sr./R.A. Draper Jr.

4133 All Stars
Designer: Mike McMahon

4134 Mike McMahon
Designer: Mike McMahon

4135 Inside Interiors
Designer: Mike McMahon

4136 McMahon
Designer: Mike McMahon

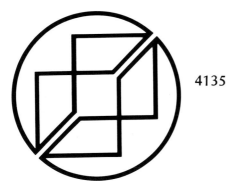

**4135**

**4136**

**MISSISSIPPI** 4137

**CAPONE** 4138

4139

Kahuku
SUGAR MILL

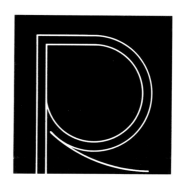

4141

Robert Powley Photography

4140

4142

ED GOLDSTEIN PHOTOGRAPHER

 4143

 4144

4137 McMahon, self-promotion
Designer: Mike McMahon

4138 Capone
Designer: Mike McMahon

4139 Kahuka Sugar Mill
Designer: Bryan Honkawa

4140 Alan Somers Associates
Designer: Bryan Honkawa

4141 Robert Powley
Designer: Bryan Honkawa

4142 Ed Goldstein
Designer: Bryan Honkawa

4143 Petersen Publishing
Designer: Bryan Honkawa

4144 Viking Travel Service
Designer: Schuller, Hawley, Candee Sauerssig

4145 North Dakota Recreation
Designer: Schuller, Hawley, Candee Sauerssig

4146 North Dakota Beef Commission
Designer: Schuller, Hawley, Candee Sauerssig

 4145

 4146

4147

bismarck parks and
recreation department

4151

4148

4152

4149

4153

4150

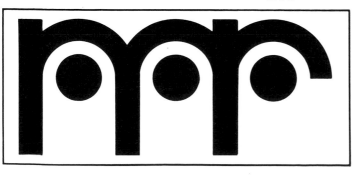

4154

*Thumbnails*

 4155

 4156

PINE GROVE RANCH

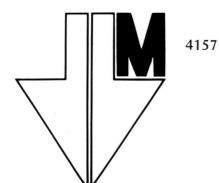 4157

4158

4147 Bismarck Parks & Recreation Dept.
Designer: Schuller, Hawley, Candee Sauerssig

4148 LeFevre Studios Inc.
Designer: LeFevre Studios

4149 Walter H. Leight Co.
Designer: Jurij Kraus; LeFevre Studios

4150 M & R Printing Co., Inc.
Designer: J. Phelpes; LeFevre Studios

4151 Dolph Baumann and Associates
Designer: Eric Madsen

4152 Minnesota Assn. for Children with
Learning Disabilities
Designer: Eric Madsen

4153 Minnesota Federal Savings & Loan
Designer: Eric Madsen

4154 Thumbnails, Inc.
Designer: Eric Madsen

4155 Fernandez & Rubin
Designer: Eric Madsen

4156 Pine Grove Ranch
Designer: Eric Madsen

4157 Mecca Ventures
Designer: Carole Poole; Charal Assocs.

4158 Atlanta Residential Developers Assn.
Designer: Carole Poole; Charal Assocs.

4159

4163

4160

4164

4161

4165

4162

**TEXAS ART SUPPLY**

4166

Systronics

**4167**

**4168**

**4169**

First National Bank **4170**

 4171

 4172

HOUSTON·CITIZENS BOOKSTORE 4173

RAGSDALE, PARDOE' 4174

 4175

4176

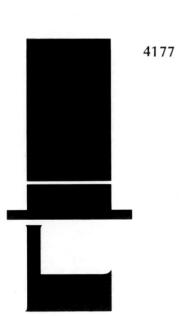

4177

4171 Lincoln Property Management Co.
Designer: Dean Harahara; Metzdorf Advertising

4172 Allen Center
Designer: Rod Lambeth; Metzdorf Advertising

4173 Houston Citizens Bank
Designer: Dean Harahara; Metzdorf Advertising

4174 Ragsdale Pardoe
Designer: Gary Coo; Metzdorf Advertising

4175 Frank Gillman Motorhomes
Designer: Dean Narahara; Metzdorf Advertising

4176 Blue Bell Creameries
Designer: Lowell Williams; Metzdorf Advertising

4177 Lincoln Property Management Co.
Designer: Rod Lambeth; Metzdorf Advertising

ACCELAGARD 4178

THE PLACE! 4179

7DAV 7 DAY
BUILDING
SYSTEMS 4180

TSPB 4181

TEXAS SOCIETY FOR THE PREVENTION OF BLINDNESS, INC.

Post Oak Lane 4182

TOWNHOMES

**4183**

**4184**

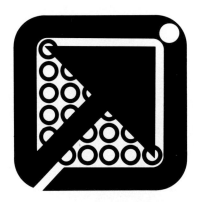

**4185**

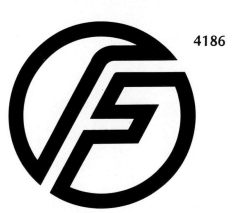

**4186**

4178 Jeanway Industries
Designer: Jim Hradecky; Metzdorf Advertising

4179 Lincoln Property Management Co.
Designer: Dean Narahara; Metzdorf Advertising

4180 Jeanway Industries
Designer: Jim Hradecky; Metzdorf Advertising

4181 Texas Society for the Prevention of Blindness
Designer: Jim Hradecky; Metzdorf Advertising

4182 L.B. Nelson Corp. of Texas
Designer: Lowell Williams; Metzdorf Advertising

4183 The Business Workshop
Designer: Diane Page/Agostino G. Unti, Jr.;
    Bentley, Barnes & Lynn

4184 Transilwrap Company
Designer: Agostino G. Unti, Jr.;
    Bentley, Barnes & Lynn

4185 Lauer & Holbrook, Inc.
Designer: Agostino G. Unti, Jr.;
    Bentley, Barnes & Lynn

4186 Fleeger Trucking
Designer: Douglas Wilson/Agostino G. Unti, Jr.;
    Bentley, Barnes & Lynn

# damson
## OIL CORPORATION
4187

# meridian
## CAPITAL CORPORATION
4188

playas del yunque
4189

# energine
4190

**4191**

**4192**

4187 Damson Oil Corp.
Designer: Flavian Cresci;
The Intermar Organization

4188 Meridian Capital Corp. (subsidiary of
Damson Oil Corp.)
Designer: Flavian Cresci;
The Intermar Organization

4189 Playas del Yunque
Designer: Flavian Cresci;
The Intermar Organization

4190 Energine
Designer: Norma Updyke/Jack O'Rourke

4191 Dellwood Dairy
Designer: Norma Updyke

4192 Kat-trene Products
Designer: Norma Updyke

4193 Amsterdam Company
Designer: Norma Updyke

4194 Pulsatron Corporation
Designer: Norma Updyke/Jack O'Rourke

**4193**

**4194**

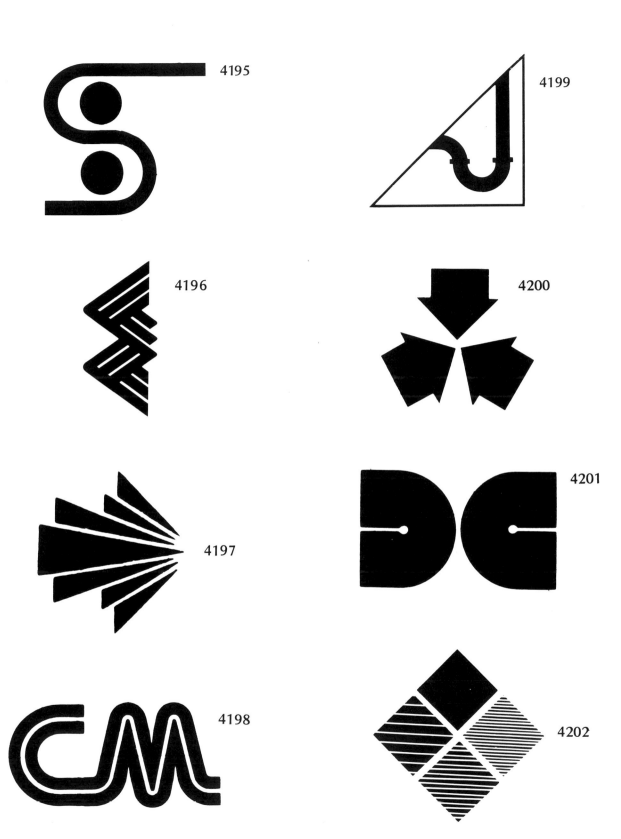

4195

4199

4196

4200

4197

4201

4198

4202

**4203**

**Ashland New Car Dealers Association**

**4204**

**4205**

# RedC★m
# READOUT

# Index of Marks

# Designers

Addario Design Associates; 176 Newbury Street, Boston, MA 02116

Ainsworth, Ray; Olinkraft, Inc., Post Office Box 488, West Monroe, LA 71291

Anspach, Grossman Inc., 850 Third Avenue, New York, NY 10022

Atvur Associates; 3057 Bolling Way, NE, Atlanta, GA 30305

Avey, Reg; Avey Design, Unit No. 5, 1040 Matley Lane, Reno, NV 89502

Bacigalupi, David, Design; 56 Adler Avenue, San Anselmo, CA 94960

Baker, E.W., Inc.; 55 West Maple Road, Birmingham, MI 48011

Bates, David; 854 West George Street, Chicago, IL 60657

Baxter + Korge, Inc.; 8323 Westglen, Houston, TX 77042

Bentley, Barnes and Lynn, Inc.; 303 East Ohio, Chicago, IL 60611

Benton, Patrick; 3141 Hood Street, Dallas, TX 75219

Bradford-LaRiviera, Saginaw, Michigan

Bradley Yeager & Associates, Inc.; Cobb Building, Post Office Box 9228, Treasure Island, FL 33740

Burlini, Al; Tom Morris, Inc., 621 W. Devon Avenue, Park Ridge, IL 60068

Chapman, William W.; CPS Communications, 2411 W. 8th Street, Los Angeles, CA 90057

Chun, Milton; 4946-4 Kilauea Avenue, Honolulu, Hawaii 96816

Clarke, Chip; 1202 Woodland Avenue, Flatwoods, KY

Company, The; 11340 W. Olympic Blvd., Los Angeles, CA 90064

Corporate Design Systems, Inc.; 210 Commercial Street, Boston, MA 02116

Cottingham, Bruce A.; 2191 Victory Parkway, Cincinnati, OH 45206

Curry, Monte J., Marketing & Communication Services, 921 Baxter Street, Suite 312, Charlotte, NC 28202

Cutler, John G.; 6921 Winterberry Lane, Bethesda, MD 20034

Cutro Associates, 47 Jewett Avenue, Tenafly, NJ 07670

Davis, Don, Design; 212 Edwards Street, Kewanee, IL 61443

Dellinger, Harvey C.; Leslie Advertising Agency, Box 6168, Greenville, SC 29606

Denner, Pat; Suite 801, Ten West Broadway, Salt Lake City, UT 84101

Design Consultants Incorporated; 333 North Michigan Avenue, Chicago, IL 60601

Design-Graphics, Inc.; 450 Tenth Circle N., Nashville, TN 37203

DiCristo, Victor; 741 N. Milwaukee Street, Milwaukee, WI 53202

Directors III, Inc.; 599 New Park Avenue, West Hartford, CT 06110

Drake, Melville M.; The Drake Office, 1409 N. Prospect Avenue, No. 705, Milwaukee, WI 53202

Draper, Robert A., PO Box 69, Ft. Thomas, KY 41075

Dunn, Crawford; RYA Graphics, Inc., Two Lemmon Park East, 3619 Howell Street, Dallas, TX 75204

Emerson/Franzke Advertising, Inc.; Merchants National Building, Topeka, KS 66612

Ensslin Advertising Agency; 102 West Whiting, Tampa, FL 33602

Equitable Graphics, 1285 Avenue of the Americas, New York, NY 10019

Estes, James K.; Roberts Hall, Cornell University, Ithaca, NY 14853

Follis, John and Associates; 2124 Venice Blvd., Los Angeles, CA 90006

Forbes, Everett; 5913 Woodstock Court, Virginia Beach, VA 23462

Franco, Jesus Emilio; Av. Venezuela No. 34, El Rosal, Caracas, 106, Venezuela

Gale, Robert A.; Siegel & Gale; 445 Park Avenue, New York, NY 10022

Gray Whyte Design House; 427 Bloomfield Avenue, Montclair, NJ 07042

Gruel, Jess; Larson/Bateman Inc., 222 E. Anapamo, Santa Barbara, CA 93101

Gutierrez, Frank A.; 2320 Sierra Leone Avenue, Rowland Heights, CA 91748

Gutke, Gordon; 569 Auburn Drive, Murray, UT 84107

Goode, Rex, Organization for Design; 1094 S. Marengo Avenue, Pasadena, CA 91106

Harland, John H., Co.; PO Box 13085, Atlanta, GA 30324

Harper + George Inc.; 18 E. 50 Street, New York, NY 10022

Henton, Tom; Faulkner Watkins & Assocs., 1900 Worthen Bank Building, Little Rock, AR 72201

Herr, Robert; Charles Crone Associates, 417 N. Boylan Avenue, Raleigh, NC 27603

Honkawa, Bryan; Honkawa Design Assocs., 1232 Crescent Heights, Los Angeles, CA 90035

Houston/Ritz/Cohen/Jagoda; 5207 McKinney, Dallas, TX 75205

Huerta Design Associates; 2500 Wilshire Blvd., Los Angeles, CA

Ichiyama, Dennis; Dept. of Design & Environmental Analysis, Cornell University, Ithaca, NY 14850

Ikola, Gale William, and Associates; 6100 Golden Valley Road, Minneapolis, MN 55422

Image Group; 330 Flume Street, Chico, CA 95926

Intermar Organization Ltd., The; 27 East 39 Street, New York, NY 10016

Jacobs, Steven, Designs; Palo Alto, CA

Joseph, Marvin L.; Joseph Advertising Design, 3404 Jefferson, Austin, TX 78703

Kaiser, Mike; Finlay Kaiser & Ballard, Inc.; Suite 999, 924 Westwood Blvd., Los CA 90024

Kannapell, Jack E., Jr.; Cobble Court, Glenview, KY 40025

Kidder Axelson & Associates, Inc.; 10544 West Pico Blvd., Los Angeles, CA 90064

Kiousis, Evan; Gregory, Inc., Cleveland, OH

Klumb, E. Christopher, Associates, Inc.; 333 East 30th Street, New York, NY 10016

Knapp Design Associates; River Forest, IL

Knight, Walsh & Associates, Inc.; 3202 E. 21 Street, Tulsa, OK 74114

Krackehl, Gene; 5-36 117th Street, College Point, NY 11356

Krispinsky, L.S.; Second Dimension Studio, 4405 Aspen Drive, Youngstown, OH 44515

LaBahn, Arnold; Peoples Gas Co., 122 S. Michigan Avenue, Chicago, IL 60603

Lake Advertising Art; 210 St. Paul, Denver, CO 80206

Landor, Walter, Associates; Ferryboat Klamath, Pier 5, San Francisco, CA 94111

Lane & Leslie Advertising Agency, Inc.; PO Box 978, Hutchinson, KS 67501

Lee, Roland L.; Ink Well, 101 N. Main, No. 3, St. George, UT 84770

LeFevre Studios, Inc.; 550 Main Street East, Rochester, NY 14604

Leigh, David; 1245 Park Avenue, New York, NY 10028

Leitstein, Alan Stuart; 8360 NW 21 Ct., Sunrise, FL 33313

Leslie Advertising Agency; Box 6168, Greenville, SC 29606

Lindsay, Dean R.; Center for Advanced Research in Design; 645 N. Michigan Ave., Chicago, IL 60611

Lippincott & Margulies; 277 Park Avenue, New York, NY 10017

Lipson-Jacobs & Associates; 2349 Victory Parkway, Cincinnati, OH 45206

Litten, Reginald K.; Sugarcreek Concepts, 221 Greenmount Blvd., Dayton, OH 45419

Lubliner/Saltz; 509 Madison Avenue, New York, NY 10020

Maccaroni, James N.; Parker Allen Co., 1309 Highland Avenue, Abington, PA 19001

Madsen, Eric; Thumbnails, Inc.; 505 E. Grant St., Minneapolis, MN 55404

Maish, Jay H., Company; 280 N. Main Street, Marion, OH 43302

Manning, Robert C., George & Glover Advertising Agency, 712 W. Peachtree, Atlanta, GA 30308

Martel, Marie; 1311 East Edgemont, Phoenix AZ 85006

Martin-Remick-Moore Advertising; PO Box 7328, 1004 N. Thompson Street, Richmond, VA 23221

McMahon, Mike; 170 Holland Drive, Virginia Beach, VA 23462

Metzdorf Advertising Agency, Inc.; 1929 Allen Parkway, 5th Floor, Houston, TX 77019

Miller, Mike; Graphic Art Services. 2141 Industrial Road, Las Vegas, NV 89102

Mock, Mark; 5030 Quitman Street, Denver, CO 80212

Morgado, Richard, Designer; 179 Jerrold Street, Holliston, MA 01746

Murphy, David M.; David Manufacturing Co., 1600 12th Street, NE, Mason City, IA 50401

Oei Enterprises Ltd.; 620 Pelham Road, New Rochelle, NY 10805

Overlock Howe & Company; 915 Olive Street, St. Louis, MO 63101

Pacey, Michael; Supergraphics, 603-990 Broughton Street, Bancouver, BC, Canada

Partain, Daniel M.; 1801 Avenue of the Stars, Suite 1000, Los Angeles, CA 90067

Paul, Rolf H., Graphics; 171 Red Rocks Vista Lane, Box 48, Morrison, CO 80465

Pelini, Lawrence E., Studio; 213 S. Jefferson Peoria, IL 61602

Penniman, Edward G., and Associates; 1537½ Pacific Avenue, Santa Cruz, CA 95060

Phillips, Wyatt L.; Marketing Advisory Group, 1354 West Wesley Road, NW, Atlanta, GA 30327

Pieslak, Jon, 224 Clarendon Street, Boston, MA 02116

Point Communications, Inc.; Post Oak Tower, Suite 415, 5051 Westheimer, Houston, TX 77027

Poole, Carole; Charal Associates, Inc. 5600 Roswell Road, Suite 280, Atlanta, GA 30342

Potocki, James L.; Huerta Design Associates, 2500 Wilshire Blvd., Los Angeles, CA

Primi, Don; Industrial Advertising Associates Inc., Station Plaza East, Great Neck, NY 11021

Purdon, Jac; 16934 Village Lane, Grosse Pointe, MI 48230

Quon, Mike; 1516 Westwood Blvd., 104, Los Angeles, CA 90024

Rabe, Peter J.; 2650 W. Mock Orange Dr., Salt Lake City, UT 84119

Rainey, David, Graphic Design; 600 Stemmons Tower South, Dallas, TX 75207

Reeves, Dyke & Co.; PO Box 27359, Houston, TX 77027

Reynolds, Stephen; 120 Brunswick Street, Rochester, NY 14607

Richards Group, The; Fidelity Union Tower, Dallas, TX 75201

Ritta, Kay; Ritta Design, 197 Sherwood Place, Englewood, NJ 07631

Robinson, George; 572 Kings Road, Yardley PA 19067

Roth, Randall R.; 535 N. Michigan Avenue, Chicago, IL 60611

Ruedy, Jeanie; 402 Oil & Gas Building, Oklahoma City, OK 73102

Sandgren & Murtha, Inc.; 866 Third Avenue, New York, NY

Sandhaus, Paul, Associates; 99 Park Avenue, New York, NY 10016

Saunders, Edward A.; 1314 Victoria Street, No. 203, Honolulu, HI 96814

Schecter and Luth; 430 Park Avenue, New York, NY 10022

Schlosser, Cyril John; 4317 York Avenue South, Minneapolis, MN 55410

Schuller, Hawley, Candee, Sauerssig Adv., Inc.; PO Box 693, Bismarck, ND 58501

Seifert, William; 350 E. 52 Street, Apt. 12-K, New York, NY 10022

Selje, Bond & Stewart; 1414 Fair Oaks Avenue, So. Pasadena, CA 91030

Sepetys, George N. and Associates, Inc.; 26111 Evergreen, Suite 320, Southfield, MI 48075

Skaggs, Steve, 546 Ridgecrest Road, NE, Atlanta, GA 30307

Smith, F. Eugene, Associates; Bath, OH

Soos, Anita, Design; 420 B Highland Ave., Cheshire, CT 06410

Spivey, Wm, Design; 3740 Campus Drive, Suite C, Newport Beach, CA 92660

Starr, E. Clark; Wells Drive, Farmington, CT 06032

Sterrenburg, Don; 8 Essex Place, Chalmsford, MA 01824

Steward, Tom; 400 Thurber Dr., W, No. 12, Columbus, OH 43215

Suggs, J. David; 1420 Lady Street, Columbia, SC 29201

Sychowski, Robert; People's Gas Co., 122 S. Michigan Avenue, Chicago, IL 60603

Sykes, David; Department of Communication Arts, Cornell University, Ithaca, NY 14850

Taylor, Pat, Inc.; 3540 "S" Street, NW, Washington, DC 20007

Thomas, Charles; Thomas Design, 822 Olive, Chico, CA 95926

Tolman, Kevin; Artra Associates, 26555 Evergreen, Southfield, MI 48076

Triad Associates; PO Box 1305, Waco, TX 76703

Tscherny, George, Inc.; 238 E. 72 Street, New York, NY 10021

Turzio, Paul; 236 Evergreen Avenue, Staten Island, NY 10305

Unti, Agostino G.; Bentley, Barnes & Lynn, 303 East Ohio, Chicago, IL 60611

Updyke, Norma E.; River Glen, Studio 26, Hastings-on-Hudson, NY 10706

Vanderbyl, Michael, Graphic Design; 1000 Sansome Street, San Francisco, CA 94111

Visual Design Center, Inc.; 108 N. State St., Chicago, IL 60602

Walker, James M.; Walker, Knudson & Campbell, Inc., 545 Rue Royale, Covina, CA 91723

Weiser, Paul S.; Kilbourn Studios, 1501 Monroe Avenue, Rochester, NY 14618

Weller, Don; The Weller Institute for the Cure of Design, 340 Mavis Drive, Los Aggeles, CA 90065

Werk, Otto; Studio Werk, Inc., 200 California Avenue, Palo Alto, CA 94306

Weston, Al; 3476 Newgate Road, Troy, MI 48084

Wickliffe, Barry; Jennings & Thompson Advertising, Inc., 2200 North Central Avenue, Phoenix, AZ 85004

Wideroe, Bernard M.; Primary Design, 1816 Wells, Chicago, IL 60614

Woo, Calvin; Humangraphic, 3776 Front Street, San Diego, CA 92103

Wood, Bill; The Design Shop, 68 Winsor Place, Glen Ridge, NJ 07028

Zimmermann, Mel; Mel Zimmermann & Associates, 317 N. 11th Street, St. Louis, MO 63101